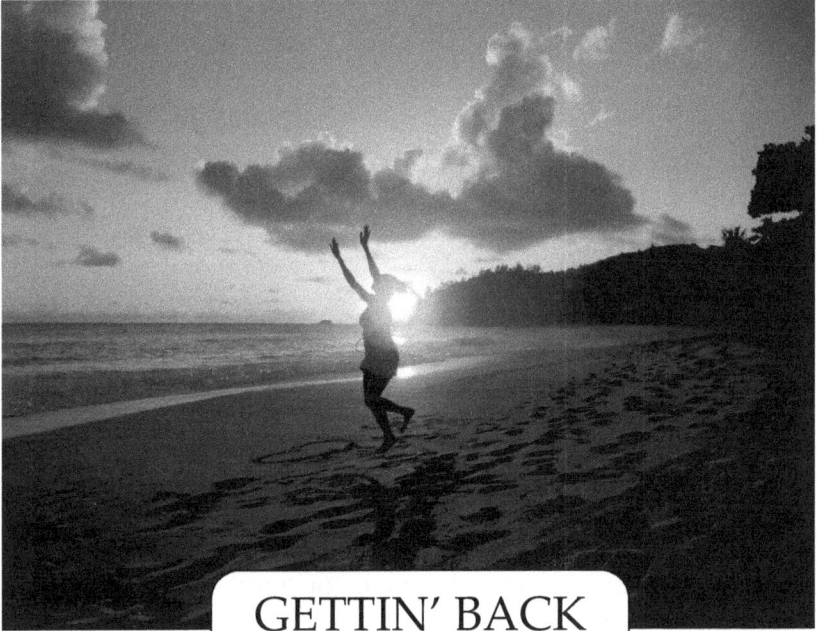

GETTIN' BACK
TO HAPPY

VALERIE L.S. ALBARDA

ISBN-10: 0615620647
ISBN-13: 978-0615620640

www.valeriealbarda.com

If you want to be happy, be.
—Leo Tolstoy

Happiness is a direction, not a place.
—Sydney J. Harris

Happiness is not something ready made. It comes from your own actions.
—Dalai Lama

Success is not the key to happiness. Happiness is the key to success. If you love what you are doing, you will be successful.
—Albert Schweitzer

God will prepare everything for our perfect happiness in heaven, and if it takes my dog being there, I believe he'll be there.
—Billy Graham

For all the happy people.

INTRODUCTION

I'm not a world renowned psychotherapist. The few things that Oprah and I have in common are limited to race and gender. And the closest I've come to a Ph.D. in anything has been staring at the plaque on my therapist's wall and wondering silently about the blood, sweat and tears that went into getting that little piece of paper.

But if there's one thing I know about, it's finding my happy. But for a while, I felt as if I were losing that one essential character trait in which I took a great deal of pride. The positive me was giving way to the negative me. Slowly but surely, this unwanted alter ego was beginning to rear her ugly head and made her presence known. How could I, the woman who constantly preached about the evils of pessimism, let myself slide down such a slippery slope of cynicism?

Luckily I had a choice. I could either give in and exist in a life burdened by my own disparaging thoughts or lighten my load by beginning each day with a decidedly optimistic slant, one that while admittedly wouldn't change the rotation of the earth on its axis could at least alter my view… if only for a day.

Armed with a touch of wit, a dab of poignancy and a splash of optimism I was determined to let it be known, one day at a time, what "Happiness is…" to me. No matter what the thought was at any given moment, I gave it free reign to spill from my head and onto my computer screen.

From an unassuming sentiment such as "Happiness is . . . being told you look like a million bucks when you feel like a buck-fifty," to something more inspiring in the vein of "Happiness is . . . reflecting on the past, living in the present and looking forward to the future," the point of *Gettin' Back to Happy* was not only to inspire myself to see the positive side of life, especially when things were not at their brightest, but also to allow others to catch that same glimmer as well—even if that muted glow is passed through the filter of my universe.

Along with many of the "Happiness is…" thoughts come anecdotal references that give a glimpse into the spark and motivation for my happiness at that time.

I endeavored to explore 365 days of happiness. In the equivalent of one years' time, a "new" me wouldn't necessarily mean a better me, so instead I opted to work on creating an "improved" me. And if by the end of the year I hadn't accomplished anything worthwhile and ended up a tortured old sourpuss, I had no one to blame but myself.

In life, we follow many divergent roads on the path that is our personal journey. *Gettin' Back to Happy* is mine. But you're more than welcome to tag along for the excursion. The more the merrier.

JANUARY

(This first month of the year was named after Janus, the Roman god of beginnings and endings. Depictions show the two-faced god looking in two directions, signifying the past and the future)

1st

HAPPINESS IS . . . new goals, new challenges, new commitments, new attitude, new outlook, new shoes, new year . . . and a better me.

Hello, new me. It's so nice to make your acquaintance.

2nd

HAPPINESS IS . . . written all over my face.

3rd

HAPPINESS IS . . . knowing that, while traveling domestically and internationally to visit friends and family during the holidays is great, there truly is no place like home.

After weeks of looking forward to this trip, I had finally left my home in Stamford on Christmas Eve to begin the holiday rounds. First stop: Christmas with my family in Maryland, followed by celebrating New Years Eve with my Dutch family in the Netherlands. Today I returned home to Stamford. Phew! I've missed you, bed. It'll be great to sleep in your familiar lumpiness after 10 days apart.

MORE HAPPINESS IS . . . landing on American soil.

Don't get me wrong: I do so love traveling. And I can take family— and all the pleasure, drama, happiness and stress that it can entail—just as well as the next person. But after being in Holland for five days, it feels good to be back home...you know, 'land of the free, home of the brave' and all of that proud American championing of sorts.

4th

HAPPINESS IS . . . setting your mind to do something and getting it done.

MORE HAPPINESS IS . . . being holed up in a Holiday Inn in East Hartford, CT in anticipation of a final big interview at the crack 'o dawn with USCIS for my hubby's green card!

The things we do for love. But I wouldn't have it any other way. My husband, Maarten, a/k/a "The Flying Dutchman", is a citizen of The Netherlands seeking dual citizenship status here in the good old U.S.of.A. As his wife, I'm all too happy to help him on this wonderful journey. So, to facilitate the process, we're preparing for an interview with the good folks of the United States Citizenship and Immigration Services.

But I'm not the only one making the supreme sacrifice for love. Our furry four-legged child, Kenji, is doing his part as well. Although he would much rather be at home snuggled up on the comfy sofa, our faithful pooch is spending the night at a boarding facility in Stamford, a place we have affectionately dubbed the 'Doggie Hilton', while his human mommy and daddy are away in East Hartford.

In all honesty, I would much rather have the three of us snuggled up together on the sofa, but since the future of my husband's green card is at stake, I'll take this temporary inconvenience over a three-way cuddle any day. Well, almost any day.

5th

HAPPINESS IS . . . a smooth interview with USCIS and the hubby being approved for the coveted green card!

It happened on the spot! Nerves were on high alert, but when you have nothing to hide, the truth is evident. The questions posed to us by the female USCIS agent were probing, intrusive and a bit odd at times, but in the end it was apparent to her that our love was true, we married for all the right reasons and there was no hint of deception. And when she declared "Approved!" with a genuine smile on her face, her countenance reflected every emotion that was welling up inside of both me and Maarten.

That just made my day.

MORE HAPPINESS IS . . . spitting, choking and "ptuuing" out my words as I make a valiant attempt to learn Dutch, courtesy of Rosetta Stone.

With all due respect to the good people of The Netherlands, my adopted homeland, the Dutch language is not a pretty one. Come on, you know it's true. With all of the unnatural, guttural sounds that have been coming out of my mouth lately, it's a wonder I haven't left the dog in a state of utter shock and fear.

Dutch people, how in the hell do you do it?

In my quest to be a good wife, I have embarked on a self-guided mission: to learn to speak Dutch at any cost. Right now, that cost is calculated in terms of frustration at roughly nine hundred and forty-three thousand dollars and eighty-six cents. I don't know how long I can stick with this torture.

6th

HAPPINESS IS . . . claiming today as my very own and beginning it with success in mind.

Sometimes we need to speak good things into existence or, at the very least, approach the prevailing moment with the mindset of success being the ultimate end result. I woke up this morning with that very thought practically coursing through my veins. It was such a simple yet powerful proclamation that I felt it had to be my fundamental thought for the day. Let's see where this takes me.

7th

HAPPINESS IS . . . a pooch on the mend.

With all that talk of claiming yesterday as my own, for all the good it did me, it did absolutely diddlysquat for Kenji. Right now, the poor baby is recuperating from a strange illness that consists of listlessness, lack of appetite, leaky eyes and an all-around quality of unhappiness that rendered him pretty much useless yesterday. It was a difficult day for him and, after watching him deteriorate right before my eyes, we had to make an emergency room run in the middle of the night to fix what ailed him.

People can argue until they're blue in the face all they want about pets being simply animals that some get too attached to, but in my eyes Kenji is more than just a dog to me; he's a part of this family. When your family hurts, you hurt as well. I paced, worried and fretted until the vet finally assured us that our little soldier would be okay. With the help of meds, he's on the mend and well on his way to being back to normal.

Thank heavens for the canine slurry.

MORE HAPPINESS IS . . . trudging through the snow with the two that I love - man and pooch.

Maarten and I took Kenji out for his evening walk and Kenji had a chance to wear his new faux shearling coat which, admittedly, is a little too big on him. Maarten seems to think Kenji looks ridiculous in clothes, but I think it's fabulous that his coat matches my very own full length faux shearling coat. Now, together, mom and pooch can weather the elements and be fashionably fierce at the same time.

8th

HAPPINESS IS . . . IHOP for breakfast on a cold, wintery Saturday morning.

9th

HAPPINESS IS . . . blah blah, blah blah, blah blah [sorry, I lost focus; hubby's gone again].

How am I supposed to react when a big black car comes creeping up to the house at five o'clock in the morning to spirit my husband away like a thief in the night? The reality of it is I'm supposed to suck it up because it's part of his job. It's called a business trip, and, sadly, this one promises to be a week-long affair.

Maarten is JFK-bound, then California-bound, and I guess I'm just feeling a wee bit lonely and distracted because he's gone once again...a week after our return from vacationing for the holidays.
On some level, I realize and understand that this is a life adjustment that I need to make. However, my coping mechanism is sometimes off kilter and I deal with the absence from a purely emotional level and not from a pragmatic one. The rational me says, "It's what he does, woman. Deal with it." No sooner does that thought crystallize in my head before the vulnerable side whines, "But I miss him already, damn it!"

Is this what it's going to be like the rest of the year? Oy vay.

10th

HAPPINESS IS . . . the calm before the storm (snow, that is).

Right now, as I live and breathe, snow is on the ground. It's the remnants from a storm that recently occurred. So now the weatherman is telling us to prepare for more snow tomorrow. We're not talking a paltry one or two inch dusting, either. They're leading every forecast with the threat of eight to twelve inches. Really? Seriously? Up to a foot of snow to come and we still have two more months left of winter.

Remind me again why I left Atlanta to live in the frozen tundra that is Stamford?

11th

HAPPINESS IS . . . progressing in life.

MORE HAPPINESS IS . . . today – 1/11/11.

12th

HAPPINESS IS . . . playing...outside...in the fresh, soft snow...with my pooch!

Do I miss Atlanta? Yes. Could I have rolled around in the snow with Kenji in Atlanta the way I did today? Probably not. While there are many places that I still miss, I can nonetheless appreciate the place that I call home. And home, for now, is Stamford.

13th

HAPPINESS IS . . . headin' to Harlem.

MORE HAPPINESS IS . . . a dog who cares.

The dawning of a new day saw me waking to an overall "uggghh" feeling. I turned to Kenji and said "Mommy has a tummy ache." As if understanding my woebegone plight and taking pity on me, he jumped off the bed, stretched like he was about to compete in a marathon, trotted down the hall, ran downstairs and returned moments later with his favorite bone, all chewed up and gnarly with mystery stains that I dare not question. Then he did the damndest thing: he dropped his bone next to me on the bed, rested his head on my tummy and gave me a look that said "Is there anything else I can do to make it better?"

Is it any wonder why I love that dog so much?

14th

HAPPINESS IS . . . on the hunt for functional yet fashion-forward boots (to match his sweater and shearling coat, of course) for my pooch's frozen tootsies!

When Maarten called me from California, I told him of my plans to buy more winter apparel for Kenji. My husband swears that the blistering cold temperatures have gone to my head and he's come to the conclusion that I have completely lost my mind. However, I can't seem to get my basic point across to him: I'm simply trying to protect my aging dog from the ravages of Mother Nature.

His argument?
"Dogs have existed for millions of years without froufrou coats and shoes."

My firm and convincing rebuttal.
"Yes, but not this dog."

Case closed.

MORE HAPPINESS IS . . . watching my neighbor's two kids attempt to slide down a small snow mound next to our driveway and, laughingly, not succeeding.

EVEN MORE HAPPINESS IS . . . receiving Maarten's Permanent Resident card (green card) in the mail!

It's official: he can stay!

15th

HAPPINESS IS . . . the warm glow of accomplishment that emanates from me.

THE MOST HAPPINESS IS . . . having my hubby home again.

Maarten arrived home this evening from California. I don't know who was happier: me, Maarten or Kenji, who ran around the house in a frantic search for his bone to present to his Daddy when he walked through the garage door.

16th

HAPPINESS IS . . . a new journey, a new adventure, a new goal - self-actualized.

I began work on a new piece of fiction this morning, which is something I haven't done much of lately. The inspiration for "Every Woman" is intrinsic. But while it comes from within, it's also influenced by my surroundings because, like the title, it is about every woman: "She is you. She is me. She is every woman." Perhaps I will enter it in the Glass Woman Prize competition that my friend Kelly referred to me. Maybe. We'll see.

17th

HAPPINESS IS . . . knowing the struggle and successes behind the desire to honor and recognize the birthday of Dr. Martin Luther King, Jr.

MORE HAPPINESS IS . . . knowing that my current state of UNhappiness will end once this nasty bug that has invaded my tummy dissipates.

Something really cruddy happened with my tummy and it began sometime last night. I'm positive it had nothing to do with the salmon and pasta mash-up that Maarten cooked for dinner. No, that's not an underhanded swipe at my husband's cooking prowess. In fact, his meal was downright tasty. Really. No, there's something else run amuck here. And whatever it is, I just want it gone before tonight.

EVEN MORE HAPPINESS IS . . . attending my first press dinner of the year.

Took a little road trip to Hartsdale, NY for a delightful Mexican dining experience. I certainly had my fill of avocado fritters, taquitos, tomatillo mussels, pollo con mole poblano, sopaipilla, black bean soup and tequila infused everything. Yeah...I'm stuffed, delightfully so.

18th

HAPPINESS IS . . . working hard, persevering and getting things done on MY terms.

So I did the whole press dinner thing, and now it's time to write the culinary diatribe. As such, I began writing my first restaurant impressions article of the year. When I get up the gumption, I plan on writing my first blog entry in 6 months, as well. Actually, I have the gumption; it's firmly planted in the initiative section of my brain. I just need to do something constructive with it.

19th

HAPPINESS IS . . . the silence AFTER Kenji's snorefest.

Kenji was snoring like a three hundred pound man. After Maarten left for St. Louis at six thirty in the morning, I allowed Kenji to climb on the bed with me.

This wasn't a first for me; I've heard the dog snore before, but the sounds emanating from my pooch were beyond ridiculous. Had I been blindfolded, I would have sworn it was a drunken trucker with a deviated septum lying next to me snoring like that. I mean, just dayum.

20th

HAPPINESS IS . . . resisting the urge to choke the life out of the snotty, rude, crabby witch at the DMV.

21st

HAPPINESS IS . . . embarking on new journeys in life.

22nd

HAPPINESS IS . . . Simpatico's first-ever Meetup event!

In a quest to mirror my former Atlanta life and live the existence of a social butterfly, I decided to start a new group through Meetup. My group, Simpatico, is for women of the seasoned variety who are searching for friendships with diverse like-minded women who find it difficult to forge lasting friendships later in life. Yeah, that would be me.

Our first gathering is a lunchtime soiree at a local Mexican restaurant today. Am I nervous? Sort of. Am I excited? Definitely.

MORE HAPPINESS IS . . . a very successful first Meetup (3.5 hour lunch) with the women of Simpatico.

So we did it! My new group, Simpatico, had our first get-together today—it was filled with fifteen diverse, vibrant women showing up for a three and a half hour lunch. I did my best to play the consummate hostess by greeting and meeting each woman. During those three and a half hours, we discovered the little things we had in common, the fascinating and divergent lives that we lead and shared lots of laughter.

This is only the first of what I hope to be many gatherings. I don't know how long this group will last, but oh what a wonderful way to a new beginning.

23rd

HAPPINESS IS . . . knowing that God is working miracles...even if you don't believe it.

MORE HAPPINESS IS . . . finishing a creative writing effort–my first of 2011.

Today, I finished writing "Every Woman." In the end it's much shorter than I expected it to be, but it says everything that I believe needed to be said. My focus was everywhere and nowhere at the same time. "Every Woman" needed to convey the strength of a woman–not just a Black woman who is representative of me, but for every one of God's creatures of the more feminine persuasion.

In this piece I have found immense pleasure; so much so, in fact, that I don't care whether I win or place in the competition with which I plan to enter. My spirit has soared just for penning it, and I share its quiet affirmation and dedicate it to every woman who has ever been and will ever be...

≈ ≈ ≈

Every Woman

Long and lithe. Pure silk kissed by the essence of satin. She moves like the finest of liquid chocolate, hips undulating and swaying as if carried along gently by the softest of breezes. She mesmerizes by her presence, unintentionally beguiling yet commanding attention. Steady as she goes, sure on her feet, comfortable in her own skin. Skin of rich dark soil, of creamy milk, of velvety caramel, of lush olive, of burnt henna, of sun-kissed honey.

She is you. She is me. She is every woman.

She is the woman seated next to you as you trudge through your morning commute on the subway. She stands behind you at the grocery store checkout, patiently awaiting her turn with quiet elegance. She is the woman who lives on the third floor in the unit just below yours. You recognize her–but just barely–as she glides past you in the austere and cold lobby. You avoid eye contact but offer a surreptitious nod that speaks volumes about your desire to covet your personal space. "I refuse to speak to you," the nod says, "but I acknowledge your existence in my world."

She smiles and her intrinsic beauty radiates outward. She is ordinary, and, in the same instant, she is extraordinary. She is the puzzle that every man yearns to solve. Pick up the pieces–of a life shattered by an understanding that has yet to be attained. Put them back together again–the fractured moments in time that make up her past but will not dictate her future. She possesses the strength of one who has been beat down by life but refuses to let it define the woman that she can become.

Perseverance. She owns it. Power. She embodies it. Weakness. She shuns it.

These are the qualities that make her human, make her real, make her authentic. Stripped of all pretenses, free from foolish pride, devoid of self-loathing. Oh contraire, she loves and adores herself. As well she should.

She is you. She is me. She is every woman.

24th

HAPPINESS IS . . . a late breakfast, and the joys of turkey bacon.

MORE HAPPINESS IS . . . Diners, Drive-Ins and Dives.

25th

HAPPINESS IS . . . realizing that Kenji's shearling coat looks more like a cape, which makes him a Super Hero Dog.

Maarten still contends that the dog, who comes with his own built-in insulated apparel (a/k/a fur), simply should not be wearing a store-bought winter coat. He is, of course, mortified and embarrassed beyond belief whenever I outfit Kenji in his shearling coat and swears he looks like a punk and, thus, refuses to step foot outside with the dog when he's sporting his outerwear. I, on the other hand, think Kenji looks positively adorable, but then again I do possess a keen fashion sense that extends beyond human accessorizing and crosses over into the realm of canine couture.

In my husband's words, "Dogs have existed for millions of years out in the wild without wearing coats. What the hell makes you think they need them now?"

It's an old and played our argument and while that may be true, Kenji has only been around for twelve years, and as his mommy, I say he needs a coat. Besides, his is the perfect complement to my shearling coat. Now, when we go out for walks together, it's obvious to everyone who sees us that we are a fashionable pair.

26th

HAPPINESS IS . . . trudging through the blinding snow on a 40-minute trek to the grocery store like Matthew Henson (and I was thisclose to waving my victory flag!) and not once falling down!

Another snow storm has begun—the seventh one to hit the Stamford area since Christmas—and the damn thing ruined my planned drive back home to Maryland. Maarten left for a meeting at the NYSE at six o'clock this morning and, since I like to display those precious wife-like qualities every chance I get, I didn't want him to risk life and limb by driving his convertible to the train station so I opted to stay put at the house for the day (as if I actually had anywhere to go anyway) and let him take the all-wheel drive equipped SUV.

This decision turned out to be a double edged sword. Once I realized that the snowflakes that were falling weren't going to stop at two inches and kitchen provisions were sorely needed, a trip to the grocery store was no longer a want or desire but turned into a necessity.

In the end, my mission was successful as I managed to lug two large bags of groceries through the blinding snow—uphill, both ways, barefoot...but I digress.

27th

HAPPINESS IS . . . looking out the window and seeing the rolling blanket of untouched snow in my garden.

Part two (or is it part eight?) of the big snow storm and 12-18 inches of the white stuff fell overnight. To repeat an overused expression, it truly did create a winter wonderland. The beauty of God's landscape is without equal.

Maarten took one look out the window and declared it an official "Work From Home" day. Metro North Railroad, the daily rail service between New York and Connecticut, sent out a test train to see how the tracks were functioning. The train derailed. Now that says a whole helluva lot, doesn't it?

28th

HAPPINESS IS . . . a slip-'n-fall on the ice worthy of America's Funniest Home Videos, not hurting myself and still being able to laugh about it.

29th

HAPPINESS IS . . . looking forward to my husband's return from a business trip, and he hasn't even left yet.

Maarten leaves today for a week-long trip to Manchester, England and Switzerland. Wait a minute...Switzerland? And I'm not a stowaway in his suitcase? What's wrong with this picture?

30th

HAPPINESS IS . . . moving forward with Simpatico–in one form or another–despite the Meetup debacle.

This may seem like a simple matter to some, but to others it is tantamount to a slap in the face and asking the recipient of the slap to pay for said slap.

The powers that be over at the Meetup organization have apparently lost their collective minds. Like a stealth fool in the night, they have taken it upon themselves to alter the appearance of our group pages without any input whatsoever from the Organizers–the very people who have to pay to 'own' the groups. The privilege, dare I say the right, to do as we please with our own groups has been stripped from our hands and, if the actions of the Meetup organization are any indication, they don't give a flying flip.

Unfortunately for Meetup, they were not prepared for the backlash that their actions have prompted. Groups are dropping from their ranks like dead flies falling from windowsills. The repercussions are swift. That's a lot of cha-ching flying out the door.

Meetup, are you listening?

31st

HAPPINESS IS . . . shifting gears, for all the right reasons, and moving forward with goals.

FEBRUARY

*(We can thank the memory of Roman emperor Augustus for
shaving one day off of February—the shortest month of the year—to
add a day to August, the month named after him)*

1st

HAPPINESS IS . . . a handful of M&M's with peanuts.

Its M&M's with peanuts. Need I say more?

2nd

HAPPINESS IS . . . living in the moment and, for better or for worse, cherishing every minute of it for the experience that it brings.

3rd

HAPPINESS IS . . . rubbing my open palms together, snickering maniacally and uttering "I love it when a plan comes together!"

What do you get the man who seems to care more about being on the giving end than the receiving end? Year after year, this is my dilemma when it comes to gift-giving for Maarten—whether's it's for Christmas, his birthday or just because. I'm usually at a loss as to what to give him.

This year, after damn near sending up smoke signals from all of the puffs generated by my smoldering thoughts, I'm planning what I hope will be a wonderfully unique Valentine's Day gift for Maarten: I'll be presenting him with a beautifully framed copy of our wedding vows. Now all I need to do is make this work.

4th

HAPPINESS IS . . . the art of preparation.

5th

HAPPINESS IS . . . witnessing a beautiful family of 7 deer walking through the snow at the back of our garden.

Simple pleasures in life tend to give us joy and bring a smile to our face. This was the case when I happened to be standing at the kitchen sink and glanced up from washing dishes in time to see the first of seven deer trot across the tree line in the garden. All females, the deer strode quickly, one behind the other, with the tiniest of the lot bringing up the rear.

I was so excited, I squealed. Just like a city girl...except, at my core, I'm not that concrete jungle girly-girl that comes to mind when you think of someone who has never seen the true wonders of nature except perhaps on National Geographic.

Yes, I have an intense problem with butterflies. And as God is my witness, I run from ladybugs. But we'll chalk up these irrational fears to phobias. I know what a rabbit looks like up close and personal; I've witnessed chipmunks at play (and, oddly enough, I've seen more than a few reduced to mixing it up and actually bitch slapping one another); I've even been privy to a possum sidling up to me (or at least as close as it could get without me fleeing in terror) and hissing as if I were invading his territory.

But there's something about seeing the familial march of deer, even after stripping away their destructive habit of eating the tulips that my mother-in-law flew all the way from Holland to plant, that brings a sense of peace and calmness to my being.

Perhaps in the spring when I look at my chewed up pot of tulips, the anger will hit me and the smile will fade. But for now, I smile.

6th

HAPPINESS IS . . . game day; um er uh, without the game.

21

I've never been much for the Super Bowl. Oh sure, there was that whole Janet Jackson/Justin Timberlake wardrobe malfunction debacle, but that had the whole world talking, not just me. But just to sit around, purposefully watch the game and actually enjoy it? No, that's not really in my blood. So as a counteractive measure, I decided for the first time ever to host my very own "Super Bowl Without the Super Bowl Party" at my home...something just for the girls.

Picture it: nine women, surrounded by mounds of food (most of which I cooked, including taco dip, crabmeat au gratin casserole, maple bacon wrapped scallops, bacon cheddar deviled eggs, chicken eggrolls and BBQ cola meatballs—you know, just a few things to tide a few hungry gals over) and not caring much at all about the Super Bowl. Instead, the day was focused on making new friends, enjoying conversation and having numerous "awwww" moments while watching The Puppy Bowl on Animal Planet, which—and my apologies here to football fans everywhere—was far more interesting!

7th

HAPPINESS IS . . . the day after.

8th

HAPPINESS IS . . . blue skies, sun shining, temperatures above freezing and seeing grass for the first time in weeks.

9th

HAPPINESS IS . . . a 4 hr. 15 min. trek home to Daddy, bypassing all of the scaredy cat white-knuckled drivers going 50 m.p.h. while clutching their steering wheels with kung fu-like grips.

For as long I can remember, my Daddy has always given me sound advice when it came to being behind the wheel of a car, especially on a road trip. His sage words have been emblazoned on my brain from the day I earned my learners permit up to this very day.

"Go with the flow of traffic," he would always say. Always.

It didn't matter if the flow meant traveling at a leisurely fifty miles an hour or speeding along trying to break the sound barrier at eighty-five miles an hour. Stay with the pack. It's less likely that a state trooper will pluck one lone car out of the bunch if the entire gaggle is moving at the speed of light.

So that's exactly what I do...I go with the flow of traffic.

Since Maarten and I relocated from Atlanta to Stamford, the proximity to Maryland has made the drive back home more accessible. After all, barring flying, I'll take a two hundred sixty-five mile drive over a six hundred fifty-six mile trek any day. Hence, my trips to Daddy's have become more frequent. And with each trip, Daddy has taken notice of how long–or shall I say how short?–it takes me to get from Point A to Point B.

Once, when I insisted to him that I'm not driving any faster or slower than anyone else but that I'm simply going with the flow of traffic, he quipped, "Then there must not have been any traffic."

I think I need to start asking God for forgiveness in advance and fudging the truth a bit. It'll make life a whole lot easier. "Guess what, Daddy? It took me six hours to get home!" It's what he expects. Maybe then he'll stop believing I'm the leader of the pack.

10th

HAPPINESS IS . . . waking up in my old bed, in my old room, in my old house, in my old neighborhood. Priceless.

11th

HAPPINESS IS . . . so wanting to be a lazy slug today but, instead, getting up, putting my big girl panties on and facing the challenges of the day.

MORE HAPPINESS . . . Home.

12th

HAPPINESS IS . . . the state of being.

13th

HAPPINESS IS . . . family time together on a Sunday morning–me, the hubby and the pooch.

Family time is precious time, and we'll try to make the most of it this morning before the ultimate time comes to take Maarten to the airport for his Atlanta-bound flight. I think Delta sees my husband more than I do.

Since Maarten will be MIA tomorrow, we decided to celebrate Valentine's Day today. The framed wedding vows was a big hit.

Oh wait, is that a tear I see rolling down the side of the face of my husband?

14th

HAPPINESS IS . . . a hint of spring in the air.

Temperatures reached over fifty-five degrees today. That's a very good sign. But how long will it last? There's a lot to be said for high hopes, but getting them too high only means they have that much farther to come crashing down to earth when they don't pan out. Damn, so much for optimism and happy thoughts.

15th

HAPPINESS IS . . . knowledge (and I plan to get some tonight in a new photography class)!

Knowledge is power...or so the elusive 'they' say. Tonight, I'm gonna get my power on! It's the first night of my photography class at Norwalk Community College. It's about time I learned how to take a decent food photograph. And who knows? Maybe one day I can rightfully call myself a food stylist.

16th

HAPPINESS IS . . . the simple things in life.

17th

HAPPINESS IS . . . turning a negative into a positive.

18th

HAPPINESS IS . . . a 3-day weekend.

It's President's Day weekend–sales, sales, sales! Oh, and the hubby and pooch, too.

19th

HAPPINESS IS . . . living to see another day and thanking God for waking me up this morning.

Do you ever get the sense that you just missed being a part of something so profoundly earth shattering that it would have changed the course of your life in a negative way? Every once in a blue moon, I wake up with that ominous feeling. It's almost as if God has placed the message on my heart that it's by His grace and mercy that I am still here. And that's the message that I received when I woke up this morning.

I awoke feeling grateful and thankful. And happy.

20th

HAPPINESS IS . . . a morning full of indulging in cooking shows, recipe creation brainstorming and looking forward to a day of experimenting in the kitchen.

Any day that I can get in the kitchen, rock the pots 'n pans, shake a few sprinkles of herbs and spices about and not blow up the stove is a good day.

MORE HAPPINESS IS . . . the surprise meal that Maarten is preparing for dinner tonight.

21st

HAPPINESS IS . . . Pepto Bismol (oh so good cheesecake, but oh so baaaad cheesecake).

22nd

HAPPINESS IS . . . branding me!

After so much time has passed, it took this long for the proverbial light bulb to finally illuminate. But once I saw the light, boy did it shine brightly.

Today was the birth of my website featuring ME. No, it's not a narcissistic rant on a cosmic level as much as it is taking my moniker, turning it into a domain and making my presence known in a sea of other www's. What a deliriously exciting feeling!

23rd

HAPPINESS IS . . . putting myself out there.

24th

HAPPINESS IS . . . setting myself up for success.

25th

HAPPINESS IS . . . seeing hard work actualized and experiencing good things rolling my way.

26th

HAPPINESS IS . . . walking away from H&R Block and not feeling like I've been violated.

27th

HAPPINESS IS . . . my hubby starting the laundry AND making an omelette breakfast for me (even though it was the most butt-ugly omelette I've ever seen, it was the thought that counts...).

Today was one of those woke-up-and-felt-out-of-sorts-for-no-particular-reason-that-I-can-quite-put-my-finger-on types of days. There's no sense attempting to explain it, rationalize it or, for that matter, change it. All that's left is to deal with it. So that's what I did.

I tried not to allow the neutrality of the day to color my world, but the subtle nuances of my discontent were not lost on my husband. So, without prodding, coaxing or the slightest provocation from me, he made an effort to sort the laundry ("Baby, can I put these new blue jeans in with this white shirt?"), then proceeded to the kitchen to alter the path of my day with the most important meal of the day.

As God is my witness, I don't believe I have ever seen an uglier omelette before that wasn't destroyed on purpose or intended for comic relief, but that atrocious looking mélange of eggs, milk, onions, herbs and ripped up turkey sausage represented more to me than the mere aesthetics than it presented on the plate. It was the embodiment of love. It was a symbol of perseverance and a show of pride from a man who didn't care that the thing he was placing before me could likely cause nightmares. He simply wanted to do something that he knew I would appreciate: my husband wanted to feed me.

Maarten stared at his creation as he placed the plate in front of me on the dining room table next to the whole wheat toast and glass of vegetable juice. I glanced down at the plate, looked over at Maarten, gawked at the plate once again and together my husband and I shared a laugh. Not a word needed to be said between us.

And then, I did something amazing: I ate the entire omelette, because it was delicious. Every last ugly morsel.

28th

HAPPINESS IS . . . realizing that while few show delight in my joy, the ones who do are the ones that matter.

MARCH

(We have Mars, the Roman god of war, to thank for this month.
Also known as 'the windy month', March comes roaring in like a
lion and goes out like a docile lamb)

1st

HAPPINESS IS . . . doing better today than yesterday, but looking forward to a great tomorrow!

MORE HAPPINESS IS . . . my Daddy calling to talk to me, just because . . .

> *For those who know anything at all about my Daddy, then what I'm about to say may sound like a complete and utter contradiction in terms, but I'm putting it out there anyway.*
> *My Daddy's not much of a talker.*

I'll give the room a second to stop spinning and take that in.

Okay, in reality, Daddy's a talker from way back in the day. He's a man who has been blessed with the gift of gab and he's a magnificent storyteller. Many are the times that he's regaled our family, friends and neighbors with tall tales of his childhood growing up in the south or his travels while in the U.S. Air Force.

To say that Daddy exaggerates is somewhat of an understatement. His stories are interlaced with knee-slapping humor, bald-faced lies and enough realism that you soon find yourself listening with rapt attention and questioning whether or not he's pulling your leg.

So for me to come right out and say that he's not much of a talker makes me appear to be the big liar of the family. However, when taken in context, it all makes sense. My Daddy is not one to pick up the phone, call one of his five daughters and spend more than a few minutes yapping away about the weather, President Obama, the latest episode of "American Idol" or anything else. This is precisely why it came as a total surprise to me when I answered the phone today and the voice on the other end was that familiar male register that I've heard and loved all of my life. And he was calling in the middle of the day to shoot the breeze with me. Just because.

I'm sure he could hear the smile in my voice. It's still here.

Just because.

2nd

HAPPINESS IS . . . swearing my dog just smiled at me.

I don't care what anyone else says, dogs can smile. It's not a reaction to canine gas, they don't have anything stuck in their teeth and, for goodness sake, they're not about to launch a full-on attack. It's simply a smile. Whether it's an emotive response or not, I can't say. I just know a smile is a smile is a smile.

Kenji just smiled at me. In return, I smiled back. I do so love having this dog in my life.

3rd

HAPPINESS IS . . . working with what I've got.

I may not have it all, but the tools in life that I've been given, I work 'em. Damn well, if I say so myself.

4th

HAPPINESS IS . . . leaving the drama of the day behind me and thanking God and my phenomenal hubby [after a marathon 6-hour ER visit, the worst migraine I've ever experienced, a morphine drip, blood tests, a CAT scan, a lumbar tap and, finally, finding relief in my own bed...phew!].

MORE HAPPINESS IS . . . my very own special version of Florence Nightingale; I affectionately call him Floyd.

I am, unfortunately, a woman prone to migraines. What began as a nagging headache in the wee hours of the morning on Thursday morphed into the worst physical twenty-four hours of my life.

Thursday wore on and several doses of Imitrex had no positive effect on my condition. All day long, my bed was my best friend. By the time Maarten arrived home from work I had deteriorated into a human mass of flesh that could barely move, talk or blink. Thinking that food would help, Maarten made a bowl of chicken noodle soup for dinner for me, but I gave up on it after a few bites.

Ten minutes later, the right side of my face felt like it was sliding off of my skull, began to tingle then went numb. Panicked, I weakly called out to my husband who was downstairs in the living room as I lay in bed not knowing what was happening to me. He in turn called my doctor, told her of my symptoms and, after being cautioned that I could possibly be having a stroke, he was advised to get me to the emergency room.

The pain in my head was excruciating—like an ice pick being relentlessly driven into my skull. As much as I didn't want to, I couldn't help but cry. It was the worst migraine I had ever had the displeasure of suffering through.

During the two and a half mile drive to the ER, every little bump in the road felt like we were falling into a narrow tunnel, spinning out of control and making contact with each and every jutting edge. It was close to nine o'clock in the evening, but I wore the darkest sunglasses I could find. The tiniest bit of light assaulted my eyes and brought new, fresh flashes of pain.

I cried as Maarten led me by the hand into the emergency room. I continued to cry as the orderly dumped my limp body into a wheelchair and sped me into the ICU. The tears didn't stop flowing, even after I reached the exam room and refused to remove the sunglasses.

I was poked, prodded, sent off to another exam room for a CAT scan and then was told that the CAT scan would only be ninety percent effective in diagnosing a brain tumor. Would I like to have a spinal tap done, they wondered. It's the only way to be sure, I was told.

Debating, debating, debating…finally, yes, I'll take spinal tap for $100 please, Alex Trebek, thank you very much. Imagine a maple tree being tapped. I wondered if the tree would scream out in pain if it had the capacity to do so. I squeezed Maarten's hand. Tighter and tighter until I thought I would pop the nails off his fingertips. The tap yielded liquid as clear as water, which was a good sign. No trace of bleeding on the brain.

Up next…a morphine drip. Count backwards from twenty to one. Twenty…nineteen…eighteen…my next conscious thought was of Maarten holding my hand as I awoke at a little past two o'clock in the morning. Groggy and disoriented, I simply wanted to go home. It would be three a.m. before my head would rest upon my pillow.

For the time being, I was free from the pain. But only for the time being.

5th

HAPPINESS IS . . . my husband.

I'm bed ridden, exhausted and musky, but my husband is still here. In my condition, we cannot share our marital bed. He wants me to rest. Hell, I want to rest. It seems the more rest I get, the more I need. And for some reason, every time I sit up, I get a headache. Except it's not quite like the migraine. It's somehow different; more intense; more persistent; direct and, I don't know, tearing within my head. It's unlike any pain I've ever experienced.

So I Googled my symptoms. Post-lumbar puncture headache.

Maarten remembers at once, but I'm foggy. The ER doctor spoke of this. Lucky me. I'm one of the unfortunate thirty percent or so of individuals who suffer from the debilitating effects of a spinal tap. Spinal tap fluid doesn't clot the same as blood does. Sometimes, it leaks. Sometimes. This time.

This leakage…this spinal fluid seeping back into the spine…this is what is causing the horrible pain in my head that won't allow me to sit up at all. I have to remain prone or suffer the consequences. In some ways, the pain is far worse than a migraine. It's totally incapacitating.

Oh lordy, this is not how I want to spend my weekend. Thank goodness for Maarten.

6th

HAPPINESS IS . . . living.

7th

HAPPINESS IS . . . um er uh, well, ya see, it's like this, errr . . oh heck, who am I kidding?!?

This morning, I foolishly sent Maarten off to Shanghai, insisting that I would be okay. He didn't want to go, but I practically pushed him out of the house.

"I'll be fine," I assured him.

I was having my first appointment with a neurologist today. She would get to the bottom of this ridiculous migraine business, perhaps give me a magic pill, and POOF! all would be right with the world. Right?

By days' end, I would end up in the ER yet again–this time by ambulance–after nearly passing out from the pain of this headache. I thought I was dying. Seriously.

What a mixed blessing it was to discover that relief would be in the form of a second spinal tap, a blood patch, to provide me with that elusive much-needed relief.

But another spinal tap? Really? You're going to bend me over, poke a hole in my spine, stick a spigot in the hole and tap me like a mighty tree yet again?

But wait...there's a twist. First I get to suffer through the drawing of blood from my arm which will in turn be squirted into my spine to essentially plug up the hole, creating a blood clot. Ta-dah!

Instant relief. I kid you not, the result was instantaneous. One hour of observation to ensure my safety and I was released.

Oh. Happy. Day. But damn, what a day.

8th

HAPPINESS IS . . . an overwhelming emotion difficult to express right now.

As I continue to recover from first the migraine and then the spinal tap headache, I find it difficult to believe that twenty-four hours ago I believed in my heart that I was dying. What a difference a day makes.

9th

HAPPINESS IS . . . "It's a new dawn; a new day; a new life ... and I'm feeling good!"

10th

HAPPINESS IS . . . taking Kenji for a walk in the garden, coming upon a huge deer, fleeing in terror and relieved that we weren't writing our own script for "When Nature Attacks!"

11th

HAPPINESS IS . . . food.

12th

HAPPINESS IS . . . the return of the hubby.

I hate it when Maarten leaves on a business trip, but I do so love it when he returns home. Especially when he comes bearing gifts! This time he disembarked the plane from Shanghai with: a) an adorable kitty bank, for the collector in me, b) a gorgeous tea set, c) a couple of CDs, and the gift that keeps on giving, d) strep throat. My husband...I think I'll keep him.

13th

HAPPINESS IS . . . Daylight Savings Time!

14th

HAPPINESS IS . . . a fluffy, clean, great-smelling dog fresh from the groomers!

15th

HAPPINESS IS . . . forward momentum.

> *Today I expanded my social media reach with the following proclamation: "I'm a twit. Find me on Twitter."*
>
> *I guess I need to brush up on the lingo.*

16th

HAPPINESS IS . . . putting good in to get good out.

17th

HAPPINESS IS . . . success as you define it.

18th

HAPPINESS IS . . . trusting and believing in God . . . but that's just how I roll.

19th

HAPPINESS IS . . . taking the hubby on a secret excursion today and hoping he will enjoy it.

Maarten is an airplane nerd...and I mean that in the sweetest way possible. So I decided to spirit him away to someplace he has never been to, The New England Air Museum in Windsor Locks, CT on the grounds of Bradley International Airport, for what I hoped would be an exciting afternoon filled with the sounds of him oohing and aahing.

It was and he did.

20th

HAPPINESS IS . . . remaining strong and pushing forward, even after rejection.

Today I received another rejection letter on my book manuscript. A few more of these lovely free sheets of paper and I will finally have enough to wallpaper my home office.

Oh well...life goes on.

21st

HAPPINESS IS . . . projects, projects everywhere!

22nd

HAPPINESS IS . . . stuff! And the many wonderful things that stuff can be. What's *your* stuff?

23rd

HAPPINESS IS . . . knowing that what works for others may not work for me, and being okay with that.

24th

HAPPINESS IS . . . two inches of snow on the ground, Spring totally ignoring the northeast region and spending 10 minutes clearing the white stuff off my car. Yay! . . . NOT!

25th

HAPPINESS IS . . . reveling in the excitement of the moment (...of shoe shopping, that is!)

26th

HAPPINESS IS . . . sleeping in late on a Saturday morning.

27th

HAPPINESS IS . . . a morning walk in the park with my dog.

28th

HAPPINESS IS . . . despite the fact that I look like a bag lady with my purple sweat pants, oversized T-shirt, holey socks and hair standing all over my head a' la Don King, I'm still feelin' good today!

29th

HAPPINESS IS . . . the long, sometimes arduous, sometimes easy, but always intriguing path to becoming a phenomenal woman. Ta-dah!

Today was a day to celebrate me. I don't think I do that nearly enough. Does this mean I strut around with my nose in the air and talk down to people as if I'm too good for them? Not hardly. It's all about feeling good about the woman that I am and not allowing anything to disrupt that wonderful feeling.

Yeah, you'd think it sounds easy enough to do and somewhere in the back of your mind you're probably thinking, "Hell, I celebrate me every day." But do you, really? Just how much do you appreciate the person that you've become in life?

Think about it, and then revel in you like no one else has ever done. You deserve it. As do I!

30th

HAPPINESS IS . . . mine. Get your own.

31st

HAPPINESS IS . . . pecan pie for breakfast!

APRIL

(This month is aptly named as etymology suggests it is derived from the Latin word "aperire"–meaning to open, just as flower buds begin to open and bloom...after the rains, of course)

1st

HAPPINESS IS . . . having my hubby back from Buenos Aires.

2nd

HAPPINESS IS . . . puttin' on my hostess hat and entertaining friends in our home tonight for dinner.

3rd

HAPPINESS IS . . . a beautiful day in Stamford and I get to spend it with my loving husband and my smelly but equally loving dog.

4th

HAPPINESS IS . . . not sitting at Firestone first thing in the morning, that's for doggone sure!

If the Dutch can design waterways that last for centuries, why in the hell can't an automaker design a car that I can drive–safely, comfortably and worry-free–for at least thirty-three uninterrupted years? Notwithstanding innovation and economic growth, to hell with planned obsolescence. Grumble grumble grumble.

5th

HAPPINESS IS . . . my little circle - the REAL one.

I know who my friends are. Or at least I thought I did.

It's a sad day when the realization hits you: the person that you thought would be the one to hoist you upon their shoulders when you needed a lift, stand by your side when you needed a foot soldier, shower you with accolades when your accomplishments deemed such merit and offer a shoulder to lean on and take a breather when life got in the way would be the one to cast you aside as if the word 'friend' held no meaning between you.

Shit happens. And so do broken bonds. It happens all the time; sometimes people simply grow apart. But it's how those disconnections are handled that distinguishes the one who valued the

44

relationship in the first place versus the one who was in it for what they could get out of it.

Guess what? All I have to give is the person that I am and all that I encompass. Other than that, I got nothing. If that isn't good enough, then goodbye.

One less person just makes my circle of real friends that much closer.

> "You cannot say you've lost a friend. If a friendship is capable of ending, it is because it never existed."
>
> ~Mayza Blanco Martinez

MORE HAPPINESS IS . . . staying grounded, but lovin' all the little blessings that life is throwin' my way, being thankful for it all and making no excuses for any of it.

6th

HAPPINESS IS . . . taking a break from the addictive madness that is Facebook.

Dear Facebook: You have monopolized my life. Because of you, I have become an unwitting participant in this lunacy that we call social networking. Between you and my beloved but equally addictive Blackberry, a sinful device which I affectionately refer to as my 'Crackberry,' I'm a hot mess.

A few nights ago, Maarten caught me updating my Facebook status on my Crackberry at two-fourteen in the morning...while I hid under the covers of the bed, all the while believing that the flimsy cotton sheet would shield my atrocious actions from his sleepy, prying eyes. If that isn't pitiful, I don't know what is.

It's time for me to take a break from you, Facebook. I have allowed you to take over my life for far too long. It's just a short break. Don't worry…I'll be back. Maybe.

7*th*

HAPPINESS IS . . . weening.

8th

HAPPINESS IS . . . learning to survive.

It's a sad testament to society when one has to force themselves to restrict the use of a social networking tool. But it really is for my own good. It's day three of being Facebook-free and, quite honestly, I'm not missing it nearly as much as I thought I would.

Maarten, who lives his life in full disclosure, seems to think something is wrong with me. He just cannot fathom why I would suddenly and without warning just give up on one of his favorite avenues to reach out to the cyberworld. Clearly, I have lost my mind, or at least that is his diagnosis of my mental state.

No, I am in complete control of my faculties, my thinking is clear and lucid and my mind is far from scrambled. For the first time since sliding down that slippery slope of the Facebook chasm, I feel free. Damn, what a liberating feeling!

9th

HAPPINESS IS . . . holding my own.

There are times when I get this feeling–it's so overwhelmingly ubiquitous that it feels as if it has always been there, will always be there and is inescapable. It's a rolling tide of emotions that wells up inside of me, overflowing in a magnificent wave of spirit that seems to scream 'I Can Do' with such force that it threatens to burst out of my chest.

For some reason, everything just seems to fall into its rightful place. It doesn't mean that I'll win the lottery, tap dance across water or bend forged steel with my bare hands. It just means that God is favoring me with His goodness.

It's at those times–when I feel as if I can conquer the world–that I am at my best.

Today is one of those days.

10th

HAPPINESS IS . . . basking in the afterglow of yesterday.

11th

HAPPINESS IS . . . repeating to the dog over and over again, "Yes, Kenji, Daddy has left for Shanghai on yet another business trip, but never fear; he'll be home soon," and trying to find comfort in the words myself.

12th

HAPPINESS IS . . . looking back on when I was a little nappy headed girl. Thanks for the memories, Stevie Wonder.

A tune by little Stevland Hardaway Judkins, all grown up and, of course, singing as the man we know and love as Stevie Wonder, came on the radio today. As I bobbed my head and sang rather loudly and perhaps slightly off key to the lyrics of "I Wish," it took me back to 1976. And just like Stevie sang in that unmistakable tenor voice that is beyond imitation, I wish those days would come back once more. Isn't nostalgia wonderful?

13th

HAPPINESS IS . . . wondering what that precise moment was when I turned the corner on a great life.

Sure, my existence has had its ups and downs, but admitting that my life today is a good one is an easy acknowledgment to make. Compared to many, I have it pretty well. That's not bragging, but merely a point of selfless pride. I have reached pinnacles that I would never have believed were within my grasp.
Do I take all the credit for that? Heavens no. But the heavens are involved, though. For me, it comes from the grace of God.

It also comes simply enough from having a wonderful man who is a part of my life. Sappy as it may sound, I do so love my husband. He's my cheerleader, my friend, my bended ear and my other half.

And it also comes from a belief instilled within by my parents, especially my mom, who told me I could be and do whatever I wanted, despite anything that stood in my way. Despite. And I continue to persevere. Despite.

14th

HAPPINESS IS . . . only three days to go…

Yes, I do countdown to Maarten's return home. I'm that kind of wife. Alternatively, it could be viewed as ticking off the number of days I have left to a) smell up the house with garlic Dungeness crab legs, b) allow Kenji to sleep on the bed with me or c) just generally act a fool until he returns. Either way…

15th

HAPPINESS IS . . . the tax deadline day that wasn't and the beauty of personally not being bothered this year. Thank you, H&R Block.

16th

HAPPINESS IS . . . writing.

17th

HAPPINESS IS . . . the return of The Flying Dutchman.

How sweet it is to watch Kenji nearly give himself whiplash from wagging his tail so furiously, then scurrying around madly trying to find his bone (and the entire time he has that big doggie smile plastered on his face) when his daddy returns home from a trip and walks into the house. It's a sign of true puppy love.

18th

HAPPINESS IS . . . the sound of uncontrolled laughter that morphs into an embarrassing snort.

19th

HAPPINESS IS . . . resisting the urge to [fill in the blank].

Sometimes there are things that you know you shouldn't do, yet you feel totally compelled to do them anyway. Perhaps it's because it gives you that little boost of adrenalin rush or makes your body tingle all over.

Late night drunk texting to your ex. Eating an entire NY-style cheesecake all by yourself. Cheating on your income taxes.

No one needs to tell you you're as wrong as a month of Sundays...intrinsically, you know. But that doesn't stop you, does it? Yeah, me neither.

Take, for instance, this hangnail. Yes, I should have left it the hell alone...

20th

HAPPINESS IS . . . being told you look like a million bucks when you feel like a buck-fifty.

21st

HAPPINESS IS . . . waking from a bad dream and being secure in the knowledge that it was only a dream.

22nd

HAPPINESS IS . . . eating super chunky peanut butter straight from the jar with my index finger.

23rd

HAPPINESS IS . . . Saturday.

24th

HAPPINESS IS . . . your husband taking one look at your freshly washed and wildly matted hair and asking sympathetically, "Is there anything I can do to help?"

25th

HAPPINESS IS . . . walking in my shoes, not yours; living my life, not yours; being thankful for my blessings AND wishing the same for you and yours.

26th

HAPPINESS IS . . . resisting the urge to place your mate in a kung fu choke hold in the middle of the night because he/she is snoring hard enough to make the bed levitate, yet you still wake with a smile in your heart and true love for the noise-making organism next to you.

I think that statement is self-explanatory and I've said quite enough.

27th

HAPPINESS IS . . . loving life, being blessed, being loved and returning the love.

28th

HAPPINESS IS . . . peanut butter...the breakfast of champions.

Not sure where this sudden stick-to-the-roof-of-my-mouth proclivity has come from out of the blue, but I've been eating peanut butter lately like it's going out of style. Smeared across bread, spread on crackers, wielding low-fat mozzarella sticks like a weapon and dipping, or brandishing my finger like a wand and boldly taking the naked digit plunge. It's been freakishly relentless as of late.

Is my body trying to tell me something?

29th

HAPPINESS IS . . . making the most of today, even as I bid my husband adieu, because the promise of tomorrow may never come.

30th

HAPPINESS IS . . . finishing what I start.

MAY

("April showers bring May flowers."
The month of May was named for the Greek goddess Maia,
daughter of the great and mighty Titan, Atlas)

1st

HAPPINESS IS . . . realizing that the best place for me to be may not be where I want to be but where I am at the moment.

It's human nature to strive to be better, to do better and to want more. But sometimes we have to take a moment to sit back and take a long, hard look at ourselves and realize that, at that moment, perhaps what we're doing is absolutely fine for that moment. Change is good, but sometimes existing as-is is perfectly acceptable as well.

2ⁿᵈ

HAPPINESS IS . . . that first glorious sliver of morning sunlight peeking through the curtains–God's alarm clock.

3ʳᵈ

HAPPINESS IS . . . the beauty in breathing.

When life's little stresses overwhelm me, I've stumbled across the perfect solution: I simply breathe. It costs nothing and it's effortless but the rewards are magnificent.

This morning I was stressed. The catalyst for my anxiety is inconsequential. What matters now is that the stomach churning feeling is gone. Poof! Just like that.

4ᵗʰ

HAPPINESS IS . . . sleeping in late and waking up knowing that God has blessed me with another day.

5ᵗʰ

HAPPINESS IS . . . feeling the love, even from afar.

6th

HAPPINESS IS . . . taking the time to know me, appreciate me and love me. It's not always about me, but sometimes it's nice to put me first every once in a while (and this applies to you as well).

7th

HAPPINESS IS . . . admitting out loud that hanging out in NYC until 2:00 a.m. is further proof that I'm no spring chicken!

Who the hell do I think I am? It's been ages since I've hung out until two o'clock in the morning anyplace that wasn't my bedroom, living room, kitchen or home office. So apparently I must have taken temporary leave of my senses since I was traipsing around the streets of New York City (and we all know it's reputed to be a city that never sleeps anyway) until the wee hours. But come on, is it any wonder that I fell under the spell and couldn't resist the lure of the city? With so much to do in The Big Apple...

Cocktails, people watching, conversation, laughter, dinner, more conversation, more cocktails, loads of laughter... Oh, my body is really gonna love me for this in the morning.

I am getting far too old for this s**t!

8th

HAPPINESS IS . . . despite the fact that I didn't suffer from bloated feet, couldn't see my toes for months, didn't experience weird food cravings, didn't go through 19 hours of intense labor or never actually gave birth, it warms the cockles of my heart to be told "Happy Mother's Day" today—after all, stepmoms are moms too.

Feeling a little slighted because it's Mother's Day and I'm not feeling very mothered yet...

Is this the normal plight of the stepmother?

I've only held the title of 'stepmom' since August 2009, so maybe the finer nuances of the role haven't fully set in yet. Of course, not being a full-time stepmom lends itself to the 'out of sight out of mind' mentality.

My stepson Robert lives in England with his mother, stepdad and two sisters, Hannah and Ella. Maarten travels frequently to be with him, while, in return, Robert only comes to visit us once a year for roughly two weeks.

Although I do get the opportunity to see him at other times throughout the year, is that two-week window really enough time to play the stepmother role to the hilt while leaving a favorable lasting impression?

I love Robert and there's no question in my mind that he loves me as well. But I wonder if I'm being selfish to expect to be held in full-time regard when I'm only a part-time parent.

Perhaps this is a question for Dr. Phil.

Meanwhile, back at the ranch, by days' end I had heard those three magic words uttered across the miles...direct from Robert to me. At Maarten's urging? Perhaps. But the sentimental gesture was enough to appease my misaligned spirit.

"Happy Mother's Day, Valerie." Out of the mouths of babes.

9th

HAPPINESS IS . . . after a bumpy start this morning, stepping back, regrouping and realizing I need to live my life as if my mother's watching.

Sometimes being a grump is the wrong way to start the day. Sorry Mommy.

10th

HAPPINESS IS . . . despite the copious amounts of pollen, waking up to a beautiful spring day.

11th

HAPPINESS IS . . . day-trippin' around the streets of Harlem, then getting my soul food feast on at Red Rooster.

Red Rooster. Hmmm...not all it was cracked up to be.

12th

HAPPINESS IS . . . feeling the joy of—wait a sec, what am I doing up so freakin' early?!?

It's five twenty-three in the morning. This is wrong on so many levels. Absolutely criminal. Where's the phone...I'm calling my lawyer.

13th

HAPPINESS IS . . . being perceptive enough to know I'm a woman of intelligence, yet being humble enough to know I don't know it all.

MORE HAPPINESS IS . . . me and the pooch having the hubby home once again.

14th

HAPPINESS IS . . . Candy Dulfer in concert tonight.

15th

HAPPINESS IS . . . being up so early that I'm going back to bed now.

> *This would be laughable if I weren't so freaking tired. Sleep was not my friend overnight. After falling into a fitful sleep, I tossed and turned all night and finally gave up the ghost. Silly me; I thought slipping out of bed and creeping downstairs so I wouldn't disturb my snoozing husband at four thirty in the morning was a bright idea. It's now six twenty-two a.m. I'm tired, my breath stinks so bad I can almost see it and for some peculiar reason my body feels like it's been stomped upon by an army of dwarfs wearing cleats. I'm taking my ass right back to bed.*

MORE HAPPINESS IS . . . knowing that genuine efforts are worth something and having an awareness that, while my arms are long, they're far too short to reach out to those who won't return the embrace. I'm okay with that now.

16th

HAPPINESS IS . . . getting on the stick (whatever that means) and getting out early to have all my important stuff done before noon.

17th

HAPPINESS IS . . . being a girlie-girl, ergo: I am woman, therefore I over-pack.

> *Getting ready for BlogHer Food '11 where I'll be heading back to my old stomping grounds in Atlanta. Gee, it's so difficult to pack with some degree of practicality. A four day trip for a gal like me requires at least ten outfits. At least.*

18th

HAPPINESS IS . . . new chapters in life.

19th

HAPPINESS IS . . . an early start to a very long day in Atlanta.

20th

HAPPINESS IS . . . starting the day off at the BlogHer Food '11 Conference at the Atlanta Westin Peachtree Hotel.

21st

HAPPINESS IS . . . my first 24 hours as a new aunt!

Welcome to the world, Timothy James Miller. At twenty-one and a half inches long, my new nephew came screeching into existence at seven eighteen a.m., weighing in at a respectable seven pounds six ounces. Well done to the proud momma and papa, my sister and her husband.

22nd

HAPPINESS IS . . . a weekend spent back "home", one last half day here, then it's back to the Albarda homestead in CT. I miss my pooch and my hubby, the latter of which I won't see until Friday.

MORE HAPPINESS IS . . . Pappadeaux.

It's not easy to watch the ones you love deal with overturned apple carts and weather the tumultuous storms in their lives. For me, it was witnessing the demise of the relationship of my husband's boyhood friend and his wife.

In life, we learn—or we should learn—not to become embroiled in the romantic entanglements of others, no matter how much we love and care for them. As adults, their lives are their own and, as such, they are responsible for making the decisions that best suit them.

Even knowing this, it was difficult for me to separate the 'caring' me from the 'mind your own damn business' me, even as I watched the world of two people that I love and respect crumble at their feet.

It took more than a little time, but I soon came to terms with what occurred in their lives—yes, their lives—and put aside a few selfish disgruntled feelings that I had been harboring long enough to re-forge the bonds that had come slightly undone with the individual that I deemed at fault.

We came together over a meal at Pappadeaux and, for me, it was one of those affirming and cathartic moments that set you back on track and make life right again. Yes, it was just a meal, but food and its transformative qualities have a way of doing that.

UNHAPPINESS IS . . . a delayed flight back home. On the bright side, HAPPINESS IS . . . a cocktail or six while I slowly whittle away the hours (and possibly singing a show tune or two in my time of self-indulgent merriment).

23rd

HAPPINESS IS . . . a cheesy turkey bacon turkey burger, done my way, just the way I like it.

24th

HAPPINESS IS . . . making a valiant effort to work at home but being distracted by the antics of the bunnies, chipmunks and birds just outside my office window—it's Wild Kingdom in the 'burbs.

MORE HAPPINESS IS . . . falling into bed completely exhausted; a sure sign that I was a hard working woman today.

25th

HAPPINESS IS . . . starting the day too damn early after having rolled out of bed for some inexplicable reason at 5:45 a.m.

26th

HAPPINESS IS . . . not having watched a single vocally-charged episode of American Idol this season.

MORE HAPPINESS IS . . . sharing laughter and conversation, making memories and enjoying cocktails over a leisurely dinner with my friend.

As I get older, now more than ever, I realize it's the little things...

27th

HAPPINESS IS . . . reuniting later today with my hubby AND pooch! What could be better?!?

28th

HAPPINESS IS . . . family time.

It's the long Memorial Day weekend and the entire family, including the dog, will be setting off on a road trip to Newport, Rhode Island. It's a first for our little trio and Kenji gets to stay in his first pet-friendly bed & breakfast. Lucky pooch!

29th

HAPPINESS IS . . . hoping the fog burns off so I can see 20 feet in front of me.

30th

HAPPINESS IS . . . giving thanks to those brave souls–men and women alike–who have served, and still do, this wonderful country. Salute...and thank you!

31st

HAPPINESS IS . . . getting back in the saddle and invading Harlem once again.

JUNE

(Juno, the patron goddess of Rome, was honored by having this summer month named after her; Juno was also known as the goddess of marriage)

1st

HAPPINESS IS . . . the look in my dog's eyes when I'm about to bless his happy mouth with a morsel of cheese.

2nd

HAPPINESS IS . . . the early bird catching the worm (and, no, I don't intend to sauté, blanch, fricassee, grill, braise, slice 'n dice, poach, marinade or otherwise prepare the unfortunate worm).

3rd

HAPPINESS IS . . . another day.

Sometimes merely waking up and being is enough to elicit joy. In its simplicity, we should find some semblance of peace in our very existence. Good or bad, we're living to see yet another day.

4th

HAPPINESS IS . . . having my husband home; 'tis a shame he's turning around and heading right back out tomorrow a.m. :-(

It's at times like this where I've learned to stop the bitching, suck in my bottom lip and accept that which I can't change. Instead, I make the most of the times that I get to spend with Maarten. True, occasionally those times are few and far between, but I'm learning the delicate dance that a Flying Dutchman's wife has to perform in order to keep herself from falling into the abyss of despair whenever the love of her life is off to fly the friendly skies. I have to suck it up.

It's a juicy cocktail swirling with perseverance, love, patience, the ability to maintain peace of mind and a spirit of sovereignty—the sheer gravity of it all could overwhelm the weak at heart.

I hope I've gotten the measurements correct; I plan to take it straight, no chaser.

5th

HAPPINESS IS . . . waking up early enough to see Maarten off before another business trip.

MORE HAPPINESS IS . . . progress (two down, six to go . . .).

Writing articles, that is.

6th

HAPPINESS IS . . . staying busy.

On what else? Writing articles.

7th

HAPPINESS IS . . . this beautiful day.

8th

HAPPINESS IS . . . living life in the planning stages; there's always something to do, to look forward to, to strive for.

9th

HAPPINESS IS . . . no longer waiting to exhale.

Why have I been holding my breath for so long? Like I've been waiting for something to happen... It's that unsettling feeling of anticipation that things never quite feel fulfilled. Looking ahead to the wonderful things to come is a liberating sensation, but ensuring that the treasures of the past are complete allows the freedom to fully experience the future.

So from now on, when I exhale, its confirmation to me that it's time to move on.

Ahhhhh....

10th

HAPPINESS IS . . . having the clarity, presence of mind and fortitude to get up and do! Thank you Lord!

MORE HAPPINESS IS . . . forcing myself to go to the gym and realizing that the effort is worth it in the end.

EVEN MORE HAPPINESS IS . . . saying "I'm glad I did" instead of "I wish I had".

11th

HAPPINESS IS . . . having my hubby home for an entire day and a half!

MORE HAPPINESS IS . . . staying inside while Maarten braves the positively chilly temps outdoors to grill fresh cod, tilapia, chicken sausage, squash, zucchini and, yes, marinated tofu!

12th

HAPPINESS IS . . . Sunday.

13th

HAPPINESS IS . . . knowing that even though the hubby isn't here, the scent of his new shampoo still lingers on his pillow to comfort me.

MORE HAPPINESS IS . . . a pooch with a good heart who doesn't want me to get lonesome, so while his daddy is away, he spent the night on the bed snoring loud enough for me to wear my earplugs!

EVEN MORE HAPPINESS IS . . . having your spouse say to you, "Baby, I'm so proud of you," and mean it. That's the type of support that all the money in the world can't buy.

14th

HAPPINESS IS . . . breaking the cycle of sabotage by not saying "I can't" even before I've tried.

15th

HAPPINESS IS . . . any day above ground.

16th

HAPPINESS IS . . . finally getting my internal engine going and enjoying a long, invigorating power walk in the park.

17th

HAPPINESS IS . . . my pooch, who cuddled with me through the raging storm in the wee hours of the morning.

MORE HAPPINESS IS . . . keeping my fingers (along with my eyes, toes, legs, arms and my butt cheeks) crossed that my hubby's plane from Paris arrives without incident in this choppy, crappy, rainy, thundery, stormy Spring weather.

EVEN MORE HAPPINESS IS . . . trying to get Kenji, a dog with no opposable thumbs, to wrap his special gift for his daddy for Father's Day.

> Kenji's special gift to Maarten: "The Little Black Book of Dog Jokes," an adorable, well, little black book full of corny jokes, riddles, anecdotes and other gems about our canine friends.

> Q: What do you get when you cross a pit bull with a collie?
> A: A dog that rips your arm off, the goes for help.

18th

HAPPINESS IS . . . spiriting my hubby away for a surprise Father's Day weekend trip.

> A surprise weekend away. Not the most original idea in the Big Awesome Wifey Book of Ideas... But you know what? I'm going to look at that as one of those 'neither here nor there' scenarios and simply take my actions as those of a woman on a mission to do something special.

> I've heard that overworked cliché, "it's the thought that counts," more times in life than I can remember, but the grains of truth in that sentiment ring true. When you give with the spirit of thoughtfulness and feeling, the gift itself should be irrelevant. Of course, a semi-glamorous overnight stay at the Hyatt Regency Long Island isn't anything to sneeze at either!

19th

HAPPINESS IS . . . extending Happy Father's Day wishes to all the Dads—including my spectacular dad, James A. Streeter, and my hubby Maarten.

20th

HAPPINESS IS . . . getting back in the swing of things.

21st

HAPPINESS IS . . . 75 minutes of power walking, run-ins with two butterflies and I didn't scream once!

22nd

HAPPINESS IS . . . knowing that crappy weather is on the way, it's about to storm, the thunder outside is causing Kenji to practically shake out of his fur and I'm still going to make it a great day!

MORE HAPPINESS IS . . . bed.

EVEN MORE HAPPINESS IS . . . the pooch on the bed with me!

23rd

HAPPINESS IS . . . deriving pleasure from the little things in life.

Being told "thank you" when you hold the door open for a stranger. A smile in greeting…just because. "Excuse me, miss, you dropped this," a stranger says to you as he hands you the five dollar bill that just fell from your handbag.

These are some of the miniscule events that occur in life that are so easy to take for granted. Every day these glorious little happenings occur and every day we overlook their importance in our lives. Without these simple pleasures, the big things would seem, well, bigger. And bigger isn't necessarily always better.

I'll gladly accept the gargantuan rewards that life throws my way every now and again. But I'll never fail to appreciate those tiny treasures that are so easily missed, so calmly swept under the rug, so effortlessly ignored. They could be my blessings in disguise.

MORE HAPPINESS IS . . . failing; at least it means I tried.

24th

HAPPINESS IS . . . knowing that, although I may take a misstep from time to time, with drive and determination, each step that I take leads me closer to success.

25th

HAPPINESS IS . . . living in an imperfect world, full of imperfect people and not expecting perfection from a single one of them, yet marveling at the expectations of perfection all around me.

26th

HAPPINESS IS . . . knowing that in the grand scheme of things I am merely a blip on the radar of life, but in the eyes of the ones who love me I am so much more than that—and vice versa.

MORE HAPPINESS IS . . . Sunday afternoon and no hint of rushing in the Albarda household—Maarten's staying put instead of dashing off to the airport for a business trip. Big yay.

27th

HAPPINESS IS . . . making today less of a chore by being–and staying–in a positive frame of mind. Mondays don't have to suck.

MORE HAPPINESS IS . . . sending "I love you" text messages to my hubby . . . just because.

28th

HAPPINESS IS . . . being compelled to do things from the heart and not acting to impress others.

29th

HAPPINESS IS . . . flying the friendly skies.

Robert's 10th birthday is tomorrow and I'm flying to Europe tonight to surprise him. Giving or receiving...I love surprises.

MORE HAPPINESS IS . . . remaining positive about meeting the former Mrs.

Welcome to the progressive family unit of the new millennium. Granted, we're a dozen years into the twenty-first century, but this is my first foray into this particular brand of conjugal territory.

My trip to England is two-fold. Yes, I'll be surprising Robert for his birthday. But I'll also be putting my big girl panties on, swallowing the lump that has been lodged in my throat for the past four years and transforming into Super Wife Extraordinaire.

In twenty-four hours, I'll come face-to-face for the first time ever with Maarten's ex-wife, Karen.

The Ex. Duh duh duhhhhh. I wonder if she has trepidations as well.

When a break-up is acrimonious (such was the case with my husband's...as was my own divorce), how do you effectively deal with the ex? It was a struggle that I was burdened with from the day I discovered I was in love with Maarten. And then it hit me: this was not my battle to fight.

If I am proud of nothing else in life (or, if nothing else, don't shout it from the rooftops for all to hear), I will tell the world how proud I am of my husband's resolve to keep the peace for the sake of his only child. His determination to remain amicable in the face of divorce is an inspiration. And after giving it a great deal of thought, I decided to walk the path of forgiveness. For four years I was angry at Karen, and for what? What had she done to me? Nothing. What occurred between her and Maarten was between her and Maarten.

So, putting my silliness aside, I decided I would travel to England and greet Karen with an open mind and open arms. Life is too short to hold a grudge that isn't mine to carry in the first place.

EVEN MORE HAPPINESS IS . . . an upgrade to business class at the last minute. Perhaps karma isn't such a bitch after all.

30th

HAPPINESS IS . . . seeing the look on my stepson's face as I arrived to pick him up at school in England!

MORE HAPPINESS IS . . . meeting the ex-wife and–SURPRISE!– having an absolutely *fabulous* time with her!

Will wonders never cease?

My worries were for naught. In my mind, I had made Karen out to be an insufferable, horrible person–practically a beast in human form. Perhaps not one with horns growing out of her head and exhaling fire with each breath, but a person that, because she was a part of Maarten's past, one who I didn't want to be a part of my future. That was unadulterated selfishness on my part. I'm woman enough to admit that, and that admission is liberating.

The words can come with nothing but truth behind them: we met, we connected and I'm glad we did.

EVEN MORE HAPPINESS IS . . . looking forward to tomorrow.

JULY

(Previously called Quintilis, meaning the fifth month in Latin, this is the month of Julius Caesar's birth and, as such, was named in his honor by Augustus)

1st

HAPPINESS IS . . . blocking out the negative to keep my life positive.

2ⁿᵈ

HAPPINESS IS . . . not living by preconceived notions.

MORE HAPPINESS IS . . . making peace with the past and embracing the future.

EVEN MORE HAPPINESS IS . . . a damn great day!

3ʳᵈ

HAPPINESS IS . . . getting back to normal.

MORE HAPPINESS IS . . . American soil.

4ᵗʰ

HAPPINESS IS . . . having Independence like no other. Happy Birthday, America!

MORE HAPPINESS IS . . . countdown to firing up the grill.

5ᵗʰ

HAPPINESS IS . . . The Smurfs!

They're coming to theaters July 29th in 3D! Once again, it's the little things...

6th

HAPPINESS IS . . . my fellow man restoring my faith and assuring me that, just days away from my 48th birthday, I've still got "it!" (cat calls, wolf whistles and honking horns while taking the pooch for a walk this a.m.) ;-)

7th

HAPPINESS IS . . . waking up early and refusing to get out of bed.

MORE HAPPINESS IS . . . a 4-mile drive home and hitting green lights the entire way!

8th

HAPPINESS IS . . . the little things that make you: laugh, giggle, smile, grin, snort, guffaw, chortle, slap your knee, hold your belly, snicker, chuckle, cackle and shoot soda out of your nostrils. Whatever that little thing is, enjoy it!

9th

HAPPINESS IS . . . keeping the complaints about my life to a minimum because I know that there are always others who are worse off than I am.

10th

HAPPINESS IS . . . taking a peek back into the past–but only for a moment–and looking forward to the future.

11th

HAPPINESS IS . . . life abundant!

It's my birthday today. I wonder if forty-eight ever felt so right draped all over anyone else before.

12th

HAPPINESS IS . . . not feeling a day over 30.

13th

HAPPINESS IS . . . being thankful that I don't have cankles.

I don't usually like to talk about the physical appearance of others. When you're a child growing up who had to suffer the humiliation of being called all manner of derogatory names, after a while you tend to understand the type of pain that negative words can inflict upon another. But good gracious, forgive me for even saying this...I saw a woman who was doing a bit of gardening this morning while I was power walking. I kid you not, she had huge cankles that were so out of synch with the rest of her leg. It was simply bizarre.

14th

HAPPINESS IS . . . losing my relatively new cell phone but having enough restraint to not totally freak out about it (not yet anyway).

15th

HAPPINESS IS . . . the Bahamas.

When I look people straight in the eye, with nary a smirk on my face, and tell them that I'm going on a week-long vacation with my sisters, invariably I get the same variety of blank stare followed closely by the one-word question full of bewilderment: "Really?"

It seems that my sisters and I are, in certain circles, considered anomalies. Sisters who actually vacation together. What the...?!?

Way back when beginning in 1991 or so I began making an annual pilgrimage, usually to the Caribbean, with two of my four sisters. Everywhere we went, the response was the same when people discovered not only were we related but that we had all grown up under the same roof and were to that day still brave enough to spend an entire week holed up in a tiny hotel or condo room together without a) poisoning at least one member of the party, b) shoving a curling iron up someone's nostril while they sleep, c) engaging in a murder/suicide pact or d) snatching each other bald.

Yes, growing up, the Streeter girls had, at times, experienced terrifying moments that crept ominously close to all-out brawls at the family dinner table, but doesn't every family engage in such dysfunctional behavior from time to time? As adults, our coping skills are fine-tuned and well-honed. We just know how to get along. Most days.

So now here we are, four of the five Streeter girls, taking an unsuspecting island of The Bahamas by storm. If you should happen to run into us on the island, please...don't stop and stare or point at us like we're circus oddities. And whatever you do, don't dare ask to touch us. We're flesh and blood, just like you.

You see, we're sisters. We're The Streeter Girls.

16th

HAPPINESS IS . . . finally arriving at Westwind II Club, Cable Beach Bahamas...yeah!

17th

HAPPINESS IS . . . being on vacation and still being able to watch the Women's World Cup Finals!

18th

HAPPINESS IS . . . getting my beach and pool time in today before a severe thunderstorm hits the island...sigh.

So much for fun in the sun, sand and surf.

19th

HAPPINESS IS . . . reveling in vacation time, but looking forward to returning to my own bed.

Vacation time is great, especially when surrounded by loved ones. But I swear to all that is just, holy and pure, it's just about time to go. I love my sisters, but if the eldest of the Streeter girls and I get into one more argument...well, let's just say that "shoving a curling iron up someone's nostril while they sleep" is looking like a pretty good option right about now.

20th

HAPPINESS IS . . . working hard at hardly working.

21st

HAPPINESS IS . . . seeing a good thing come to an end, and being okay with that.

The Streeter Girls vacation is nearing its end. As much as I have enjoyed my time with my sisters, there has also been stress involved, too. I say this with the utmost love and respect: one week is almost too long! It'll be good to get back home to my little family unit.

22nd

HAPPINESS IS . . . daydreaming.

23rd

HAPPINESS IS . . . um er uh, lemme get back to you on this one.

Goodbye Bahamas...so long, farewell and adieu. You've taken good care of me all week with calming breezes, warm and comforting waters, friendly people, cocktails galore and, of course, cuisine fit for a queen. Despite the ups (there were many) and the downs (who's counting?!?), it's a shame it has to come to an end. But don't despair for I shall return. One day. Soon.

Parting is such sweet sorrow...

24th

HAPPINESS IS . . . basking in the memories of a great vacation, but glad to be back home with the pooch! (Too bad the hubby is MIA in Buenos Aires...).

25th

HAPPINESS IS . . . having the fortitude to push forward when life is trying to drag you backwards.

26th

HAPPINESS IS . . . waking up this morning and affirming that today is going to be a great day.

27th

HAPPINESS IS . . . fueling my future with the positive energy of today.

28th

HAPPINESS IS . . . dismissing the second guessing and trusting the decisions I make.

MORE HAPPINESS IS . . . appreciating the beauty of true friendship and ignoring those whose motives are less than pure.

29th

HAPPINESS IS . . . 1) identifying a goal; 2) setting the goal; 3) achieving the goal; 4) repeating steps 1-3.

30th

HAPPINESS IS . . . waking up next to the love of my life–my hubby.

As I begin my day, I do so with a glowing sense of pride. Not a boastful pride firmly entrenched in me but, rather, a dignified view of respect for Maarten who, for the second year in a row, has been nominated for the International Marketer of the Year Award. He must be doing something right in the position that he took the helm of a mere two years ago. Beaming…

MORE HAPPINESS IS . . . seeing that Kenji is so happy to have his daddy home that he's been shadowing him all day.

31st

HAPPINESS IS . . . being a problem solver, not a troublemaker; saying "I can" instead of "I can't"; facing life head-on instead of burying my head in the sand; living my life in my shoes and not trying to live vicariously through yours. In short, being me.

It was just something that needed to be said. There's no pretense to the person that I am. For me to make the proclamation that 'I try to be genuine' feels farcically disingenuous. When a person is being their own self, there's no need to struggle at being the you that you truly are. The person that you are—those intrinsic qualities that make up your individuality—don't need to be rehearsed, studied or practiced.

As time goes on I'll continue to do me, to celebrate me, to be me.

AUGUST

(Augustus, the first Roman emperor, was honored with the naming
of this month because of several fortunate events throughout
his life which occurred during the month)

1st

HAPPINESS IS . . . being caught up in the beauty and love that is
my two-year anniversary.

2nd

HAPPINESS IS . . . a state of mind.

MORE HAPPINESS IS . . . Europe-bound.

3rd

HAPPINESS IS . . . touching down on Netherlands soil.

4th

HAPPINESS IS . . . loving the wonderful family I've been blessed with, both at home and abroad.

MORE HAPPINESS IS . . . singing "Rain, Rain, Go Away!" loud, off-key and with gusto!

5th

HAPPINESS IS . . . deep reflection—Mother Nature conspired against me, and now the cootie gods have also joined in on the fun. I now have whatever cold it was that Maarten had. Great. What's next?!?

6th

HAPPINESS IS . . . practicing the art of mind over matter: I am not sick; I am not sick; I AM not sick!

Yeah, I'm sick.

7th

HAPPINESS IS . . . less "uggghhhh" and more "ahhhh".

...which is an extremely difficult stance to take once you've had a bug in your pants.

I tried. God knows I did. Camping is not my thing. The thought of sharing my space with anything other than a human, my dog or any other pet just willies me out. So imagine my complete horror when, after a lovely day of wandering around the campgrounds, spending time with the entire Dutch contingent and a nice fireside barbeque, Maarten and I retire back to our tiny home-away-from-home caravan and, as I'm undressing, an earwig falls out of my pants.

DISCLAIMER: Google this bug at your own risk and with extreme caution. If you're anything like me–a/k/a you suffer from an intense, near-paralyzing fear of bugs–you'll think there's something crawling on you for days after seeing a photo of an earwig. I take no responsibility for any fainting spells, blood curdling screams or ripping off of clothing.

Given my proclivity for either a) fleeing in terror at the sight of a bug, b) yelling at the top of my lungs as if I'm in the throes of being murdered, or c) both, Maarten was duly impressed that neither act was carried out when I stepped out of the tiny bathroom with a look of sheer terror on my face.

My terrible cold had rendered me almost devoid of energy and I was spent. There was no more oomph left in me and I couldn't even manage a shrill shriek.

"Baby, a bug just fell outta my pants," I croaked as I pointed in the direction of the bathroom.

Lifesaver that he is, my husband deftly swept into the bathroom, pinched the bug between his thumb and index finger and flicked it out the window. Having dispatched of the hideous and deadly creature–yes, in my world, bugs are far worse than any horror movie I've ever seen–he stared at me as I sat on the edge of the tiny bed shaking.

"I'm proud of you, baby. I'm surprised you didn't go tearing out of here."

Any other day of the week, I clearly would have run through the bathroom wall, leaving only an outline of my fleeing form, just like in a cartoon.

Uggghhhh. I am so ready for this camping trip to be over.

8th

HAPPINESS IS . . . whether good or bad, losing track of my days while I'm on vacation.

MORE HAPPINESS IS . . . the sun.

EVEN MORE HAPPINESS IS . . . living my life vertically, not horizontally.

Epiphanies can hit you at the damnest of times.

I'm in the middle of a campground in Baarn, in the province of Utrecht in The Netherlands. The sun has disappeared, a horrible cold has been holding me hostage for the past few days and, this being smack dab in the middle of nature, there are at least a gazillion bugs crawling and flying around outside that refuse to believe me when I tell them that, no, I am not their dinner for the evening.

But in the midst of all of this relatively mild chaos, I decided that life is much better when I'm moving upward instead of being stagnant, complaining about what's not right about life and making everything right about it.

Of course, I'm also influenced by the mere thought of a pet project I'm working on that I hope will change the way at least a few people think about their love of food...

9th

HAPPINESS IS . . . not waiting for good things to happen but playing a role in making them happen.

10th

HAPPINESS IS . . . bidding adieu to the campgrounds and heading back to civilization!

If I didn't think it would hurt my in-laws' feelings, I swear I'd start doing cartwheels, back flips and somersaults while high-fiving every person I saw in celebration of leaving the campgrounds. It's been real, but it's also been the bane of my existence for the past five days.

On the upside, I've added eighty-four new words and phrases to my Dutch language arsenal during the camping trip. Not too shabby, eh?

Civilization, here I come!

11th

HAPPINESS IS . . . taking stock in your life and realizing that, despite the ups and downs...the successes and failures...the good and the bad...weathering the tribulations that make you stronger or momentarily succumbing to your weaknesses, it's a pretty good life after all. So go ahead . . . celebrate you!

12th

HAPPINESS IS . . . positive thoughts in a negative world.

MORE HAPPINESS IS . . . lekkerbekje for lunch.

Lekkerbekje, a Dutch delicacy, is a fried haddock filet. While out scavenging around for shoes for Robert after a trip to the "kassboer" (cheese farmer) in Sassenheim, we stopped by the fishmonger in a quaint shopping village (yes, they really do exist) for smoked salmon for Oma and Opa for lunch.

Lekkerbekje: I. Want. More.

13th

HAPPINESS IS . . . the gift of friendship.

14th

HAPPINESS IS . . . knowing that while traveling can be good for the soul, there certainly is no place like home. Here I come, America!

15th

HAPPINESS IS . . . progress.

16th

HAPPINESS IS . . . lying next to a dog that's passing gas yet has the audacity to look at me like I did it.

17th

HAPPINESS IS . . . reflecting on the past, living in the present and looking forward to the future.

18th

HAPPINESS IS . . . aging gracefully.

19th

HAPPINESS IS . . . the unique beauty of secrets.

For months now, I've been lying to my husband.

What kind of low-down, scheming wife admits out loud for God and everybody to hear that she's a big fat liar? The kind who has been secretly planning a surprise 50th birthday party for her husband.

While Maarten's 50th isn't until the 21st of this month, I've planned a big shindig for him tomorrow evening complete with heavy hors d'oeuvres, friends, lots of cocktails, music and me! This whole underhanded cloak-and-dagger routine has been killing me, but this is one secret that is well worth keeping!

20th

HAPPINESS IS . . . tumbling back into bed.

MORE HAPPINESS IS . . . watching the day unfold.

> *It's party time! While there was at least one major hiccup–my entire family, who was making the trek from Maryland to Stamford, was stuck in horrible traffic that turned a four and a half hour trip into a nine hour journey–the party was a rousing success. Eventually, all but two guests arrived, Maarten was surprised beyond his wildest imagination and, for my efforts, I finally fell into bed at three in the morning.*

21st

HAPPINESS IS . . . knowing that it takes only one day to change all the rest.

22nd

HAPPINESS IS . . . the day after the day after.

23rd

HAPPINESS IS . . . making peace with my inner self and realizing the "me" that I am isn't such a bad "me" after all.

24th

HAPPINESS IS . . . finding balance.

I'm juggling a lot: trying to finish writing a manuscript by the end of the month, dedicating myself to writing one article a week for Stamford Patch and launching my F.O.O.D. initiative.

Phew! Being a multitasking phenom takes a lot of work.

25th

HAPPINESS IS . . . realizing that I'm turning into my mother...and being perfectly fine with this epiphany.

MORE HAPPINESS IS . . . doing.

Today I unleashed F.O.O.D.™ upon an unsuspecting world. F.O.O.D.™, an acronym that I coined and subsequently trademarked, was born out of my wandering eye.

When dining out, I have a tendency to lose all semblance of concentration when a waiter strolls anywhere near me with a plate of food. It's actually a fascinating transformation to watch unfold. I could be deep in conversation when suddenly all manner of awareness ceases. A temporary trance overtakes me as my eyes follow a plate, bowl or cart of food, usually until it's out of sight. Then, just as suddenly, I'm back in the real world, resuming the tête-à-tête as if nothing out of the ordinary had just occurred.

This bizarre behavior has freaked out more than a few of my dining companions, who have been mistakenly under the impression that I was in the midst of a vicious seizure of some sort and at least one person actually tried to shove a popsicle stick in my mouth to keep me from swallowing my tongue.

I was certain that this affliction, which didn't yet have a name, was something that I had in common with others, except it was shared in silence. How many other people were zoning out, ogling plates of food and devouring them with their eyes?

F.O.O.D.™ was born. Food Ocular Obsessive Disorder.

I'm still waiting for the droves of individuals suffering from F.O.O.D.™ to bravely step forward, out of the shadows of shame, and say to the world, "Hi, my name is [fill in blank] and I suffer from F.O.O.D."

It's okay to admit it. I'm here for you.

26th

HAPPINESS IS . . . staying strong, holding my head high and letting my haters be my motivators.

I must admit today I am feeling a bit perplexed and betrayed. You expect those who may not have a fondness for you to be somewhat lackluster in their show of support. But for those more trusted individuals, the ones you count as friends, to ignore the advancements you're trying to make in life?

Silence is golden.

Unfortunately, some people would rather remain silent than to give even the slightest hint of praise. It fills me with a special brand of despondency because it feels like the ones who I thought were true friends, aren't. But I've been down this road before. Out of sight out of mind, as it were. It's a little depressing, but this temporary state is also a blessing in disguise because it serves as a motivation tool for me.

I don't want this to be a roller coaster ride. I'm getting off at the next stop.

MORE HAPPINESS IS . . . finished!

I've finally finished my Johannesburg manuscript! Wow...this feels exceptionally satisfying. Now comes the really difficult part: major editing. Luckily I have a professional editor tapped for the overall process, but since this book is my baby, the time I put into it makes the outcome all the more sweet.

27th

HAPPINESS IS . . . battening down the hatches, hunkering down and prepping with my little family unit.

Hurricane Irene is on her way. Damn that tempestuous storm. Yesterday morning there was a soft breeze reminiscent of the islands, the humidity was low and the sun was casting its gorgeous rays outward, reaching into darkened nooks and crannies and brightening even the murkiest of spaces. It truly was the calm before the storm.

Today, the grocery stores look like battle zones, the lines at the gas stations are snaking out into the streets, low lying areas of NYC are under orders of mandatory evacuation and we're expecting destruction and calamity to interrupt the relative tranquility all along the East coast. Preparedness is the key. I pray for a safe outcome.

This impending hurricane scares me. I think it's even had an impact on Kenji, as well. As Maarten was making his way through the garage to the car which was parked in the driveway, Kenji actually yelped/cried. I'd never heard this particular sound come out of my dog before and it was so touching to witness. My mommy instincts told me he was afraid and didn't want Maarten to leave. So now Daddy and Pooch are in the car running errands together on a Saturday morning.

MORE HAPPINESS IS . . . being fortunate enough to have a wonderful hubby who accepts, without question or complaint, my frequent moments of goofiness.

Sometimes I just sort of zone out and will say or do something completely goofy and contrary to my normal sane self. Maarten finds this trait endearing, as only a husband can.

28th

HAPPINESS IS . . . by the grace of God.

At 10:00 a.m. I'm praying the worst of Hurricane Irene, which lost a bit of her oomph but still battered the area in the wee hours of the morning, is over. It's been downgraded to a tropical storm and, so far, we haven't lost power nor have we sustained any damage. Praise God.

Unfortunately, all around us, as close as a half a mile away, homes are without electricity, trees are downed, power lines are ruptured and the area is in for a major clean-up effort.

29th

HAPPINESS IS . . . what a difference a day makes.

Yesterday Hurricane Irene morphed into a tropical storm and blew through Stamford. Today, it's clear azure skies and crisp Autumn-like weather. That's the awesome power of God, folks.

30th

HAPPINESS IS . . . the restorative powers of an apology.

31st

HAPPINESS IS . . . recognizing that the mistakes I make today are a lesson for tomorrow.

SEPTEMBER

(Also known as the "harvest month," the word September is derived from the old Roman word 'septem' because it was the seventh month of the Roman calendar)

1st

HAPPINESS IS . . . fooling myself into believing that a big slice of Brownie Sundae Cheesecake has zero calories, but staying away from it anyway!

MORE HAPPINESS IS . . . dancing like nobody's watching.

2nd

HAPPINESS IS . . . leaving one day behind and starting anew — as life should be.

3rd

HAPPINESS IS . . . paying my friendship dues with my heart and not with empty lip service.

4th

HAPPINESS IS . . . taking a bite out of The Big Apple.

MORE HAPPINESS IS . . . falling off the South Beach Diet wagon and lovin' rolling around in the shame of it all!

5th

HAPPINESS IS . . . those brief moments in time when everything just feels right.

6th

HAPPINESS IS . . . rising above.

MORE HAPPINESS IS . . . F.O.O.D.™.

Today is the unveiling of my F.O.O.D. ™ t-shirt design.

7th

HAPPINESS IS . . . trying.

8th

HAPPINESS IS . . . using the setbacks in life as motivation to move forward.

9th

HAPPINESS IS . . . the individual people, places and memories that make up the wonderful puzzle that is my life.

10th

HAPPINESS IS . . . knowing that it's okay to observe in life, but the ones who can truly speak from experience are the ones who *do*.

11th

HAPPINESS IS . . . remembering 10 years ago today and honoring it with the utmost respect.

12th

HAPPINESS IS . . . jumping over life's hurdles while endeavoring to keep a smile on my face.

13th

HAPPINESS IS . . . putting your best foot forward.

MORE HAPPINESS IS . . . not just one but two slices of cake.

14th

HAPPINESS IS . . . rolling, rolling, rolling...

MORE HAPPINESS IS . . . commencing with the 3rd...

Today marks the beginning of work on "Gettin' Back to Happy," which, when finished, will be my third completed book. It feels great to have forward momentum in life.

15th

HAPPINESS IS . . . accepting myself as a person who is flawed until I can claim to be blemish-free.

16th

HAPPINESS IS . . . pushing through the feelings of discouragement and disappointment and persevering.

There's a cacophony of emotions that are tied up in feelings. But should we, as caring human beings, be wrong for worrying about the well-being of others? I haven't heard from a friend who I last saw on August 20. Is she alive? Dead? Hiding out? Has she decided that she just doesn't want to be friends anymore and is refusing to answer my numerous emails, phone calls to a full voice mailbox and texts? The mystery lingers.

17th

HAPPINESS IS . . . realizing that my actions are a reflection on me so I always strive for a respectable mirror image.

Sometimes I have to stop, think and remind myself that people are very perceptive and people are watching. They pay close attention to the things you do and say.

If I expect to earn someone's respect, I must offer the same in kind. If I want people to trust and believe that I am an inherently good person, that has to be reflected in my true actions and the way in which I conduct myself. I don't do this for the sake of putting on a show but as a mirror image of the woman I am intrinsically.

18th

HAPPINESS IS . . . gentle words.

Admittedly, I have a knack for well-placed harsh words that can be biting and, at times, bordering on acerbic. Unfortunately, I'm not always totally cognizant of the damaging effect of these words even as they come flying out of my mouth. Sometimes my husband is the one who can lay claim to suffering because he's usually the one close enough to be on the receiving end. (Proximity is a bitch, isn't it?)

In these moments of unsavory behavior, I honestly mean my husband no harm. So when my verbal tirades go for the jugular and I realize this (either through my own 'ah-hah' light bulb moment or when Maarten just comes out and tells me), I practice the art of correction, which includes an apology based on sincerity, not lip service. I know when I'm being a bitch and I'm just bitchy enough to admit it.

Valerie and stress don't go well in the same sentence, and my coping mechanism is sometimes a corrosive pill which I don't want to force anyone to swallow.

Gentle words.

19th

HAPPINESS IS . . . loving the here and now, but not being afraid to strive for more.

MORE HAPPINESS IS . . . not allowing the broken bonds of friendship to destroy my belief in the beauty of true friendship.

I have tried on numerous occasions to reach out to someone who I considered a friend. Emails, phone calls, text messages–almost a month of queries and in return almost a month of no contact. I guess it's true what is said: "No good deed goes unpunished." My concern for this person—especially given the relationship in which she was involved and the dubious nature of her boyfriend's character (as told to me in her own words)—caused me to worry for her ultimate safety. And for this level of care and concern my reward was to be called 'strange'.

It saddens me, but it illuminates the true friendship—or lack thereof—that we had. However, this is not enough to cause me to believe that friendships are not worth cultivating and nurturing. They are. A true friend knows this and doesn't mock the concern of others.

20th

HAPPINESS IS . . . cortisone.

Plantar fasciitis has struck again. One morning three years ago, just before going on vacation to Cairo, I awoke to an incredible pain in the heel of my right foot. I went to a podiatrist and was diagnosed with the dreaded plantar fasciitis. With the help of heavy meds (800 milligrams of ibuprofen three times a day) and a night splint, the ailment finally dissipated after two years.

In August, while on the camping trip gallivanting through the woods in Baarn, The Netherlands, somewhere along the line I just flat out overdid it. Fast forward two weeks later. I awake to that same excruciating pain...this time in my left foot. In three days I'm supposed to leave to go on vacation to Barbados. It's not my desire to limp around for an entire week because I'm in too much pain not to walk like Lerch.

A trip to the podiatrist, a prescription for an NSAID and one painful shot of cortisone directly into the heel of my foot and now all is right with the world. For now. I hope it lasts.

MORE HAPPINESS IS . . . knowing that when you give bad, you eventually get bad in return; that's why I try to give–and live–good.

21st

HAPPINESS IS . . . walking the walk; talking the talk.

22nd

HAPPINESS IS . . . letting go of the past, unless it enhances the future.

23rd

HAPPINESS IS . . . oh wait, its 5:30 in the morning and I'm already showered, dressed and on my way to the airport; what's so damn happy about it?

Today we're off to Barbados!

MORE HAPPINESS IS . . . wondering how my sweet, caring, globetrotting hubby ever manages to travel and make it to his destinations without me.

Traveling by Metro North train, we reached the Harlem & 125th station where we jumped into a taxi to whisk us away to the airport. Maarten gave the driver instructions and we were on our way. When we arrived at the airport, my bullshit-o-meter wasn't fully operational. It wasn't until the driver slowly crept up to the American Airlines terminal that I began to see signs: "LaGuardia Airport

Marketplace." I saw the signage several times before my BS-o-meter kicked into high gear. Surprised, I turned to Maarten.

"LaGuardia? I thought we were leaving from JFK?"

My loving but stupefied husband stared at me, then uttered, "JFK?" He reached for his phone and pulled up the flight confirmation email.

"Uh, driver, we're supposed to be going to JFK. Sorry."

I didn't say a word; I merely stared out the window, too afraid of what manner of profanity could potentially fly out of my mouth if I dare spoke.

My husband...despite it all, I still think I'll keep him.

24th

HAPPINESS IS . . . the melodic song of the crickets...the soothing sounds of the waves crashing ashore...basking in the golden rays of the sun...Barbados.

25th

HAPPINESS IS . . . snoring like a freight train for all the right reasons.

26th

HAPPINESS IS . . . the art of exploration.

27th

HAPPINESS IS . . . putting out in the universe what I hope to get in return: respect, love, laughter and more.

Reflecting on life once again. I'm simply trying to be a better person, and I realize that to do that I have to be that.

28th

HAPPINESS IS . . . looking beyond the false boundaries of my perceived limitations and striving to do more.

29th

HAPPINESS IS . . . loving your own little corner of the world so much that you never want it to end; so go ahead...lick the plate of life clean!

30th

HAPPINESS IS . . . the end of Baconfest 2011. My heart will thank me later.

*Since I've been in Barbados, something strange has come over me.
I've been eating pork bacon like it's about to be outlawed. I'm not one
to just sit around and eat pork and I haven't really done so willingly
and in such abundance for about twenty-four years.*

So why this sudden affinity for pork bacon?

*Anyone's guess is as good as mine. I've eaten upwards of two dozen
slices a day. That's absolutely ridiculous. And, surprisingly, not one
single time have I suffered from a headache. I'm not sure what the
secret is, but whatever they've done to this bacon in Barbados, it
cannot–I repeat, CANNOT–follow me back to Stamford.
Remember...I am not a pork eater.*

❧ ❧ ❧

"My Brief But All-Consuming Fling With Pork Bacon"

Bacon.

To some, simply uttering that one word elicits goofy grins, licking of
lips and rubbing of bellies. I've come to learn that people *love* bacon.
Now, while I'm a turkey bacon aficionado, some may consider this
particular strip of poultry to be an affront as it dares bare the same
moniker as bacon. I, however, don't indulge in pork so the
substitution of the gobbling imposter was a natural choice for me.

Having said that, I find myself to be somewhat of an anomaly. This
past week while vacationing on the lovely island of Barbados I began
eating pork bacon like it was about to be stricken from the human
lexicon. It appears I totally fell off the wagon...so much so that I was
trapped under the crushing blows of the wagon wheels and didn't
seem to care one iota.

Why, you ask?

I have no earthly idea. I haven't willingly consumed pork in mass
quantities since approximately 1988 or so. And while it's true that I
have, on occasion, indulged in bits and pieces of pork-infested meals
during the press dinners that I attend, I consider that to be an on the
job hazard. After all, as a food writer, how else can I intelligently and

knowledgeably write about the food if I have no idea what it tastes like?

I'm still not sure what the good people of Barbados—in particular, the staff at Fairmont Royal Pavilion—did to that helpless bacon. At first, I thought perhaps it was pork of the uncured variety until I realized that uncured bacon could still contain salt. That just flies in the face of my theory that the bacon was uncured in the first place because, after devouring as many as two dozen slices of the killer swine in one day, a headache escaped me. One of my sisters eats a couple of slices and she's claiming she has a migraine or brain tumor. So why was I spared the same fate?

Beats me.

I know, I know. Bacon is notorious for hiking up the cholesterol. And I may as well just slap a pack of bacon on my hips and butt 'cause I know that's exactly where it's going after I eat it. But beyond a shadow of a doubt, I could not contain myself. The thoughts were so extreme that I was beginning to think that when I met my untimely demise, I wanted to be sure that wherever I ended up, pork bacon would be on the menu.

This is just wrong.

I. Don't. Eat. Pork.

But I'll be damned if every day I was at that luscious breakfast buffet piling on the pork. There was bacon in my omelette followed by eight slices of bacon on the side. I even had the audacity to stuff bacon into a plastic baggie, take it back to our room and, at lunch, indulge in a homemade club sandwich. I couldn't get enough of the stuff.

My first thought was *I need therapy*. My husband was convinced that it was all psychological. And it was. But I blame Barbados. The salt air maybe, or perhaps the tranquil and soothing locale made me totally forget who in the hell I was and, no, I am *not* one to indulge in pork.

But all of that logic was conveniently forgotten as I ate bacon at every opportune moment. I went to sleep dreaming about bacon and the dream was fulfilled at breakfast. I wanted it all the time— breakfast, lunch and dinner. I wanted it between two slices of bread, on top of pizza, hidden inside a mound of spinach. It was totally ridiculous.

I was a shameless bacon hussy. I was addicted. *Pssst, Mister, I'll trade you my car for a few strips of bacon.*

And then, just as suddenly as the onset of baconfest had reached epic proportions, it was gone. But not without some help and a strong will. I was determined to live by the island rule: What happens on Barbados stays on Barbados.

I had resolved to let the bacon fetish remain at the lovely resort. Curses to Fairmont Royal Pavilion for introducing me to that tempting, crispy, greasy bacon.

It's been four days since I left Barbados and bacon. Not once, since I've been back home, have I wanted to run to the kitchen, fry up a pound of bacon and eat it like I had lost total control of my senses. Not once. I'm proud of that. I told my husband that pork bacon would not ruin my life. And after nearly twenty-four years of being relatively bacon-free, why mess up a good thing?

OCTOBER

(Part of the harvest season, October, the name of which originates from the word "octo" meaning eight [it was the eighth month on ancient Roman calendars], is when Autumn is in full swing)

1ˢᵗ

HAPPINESS IS . . . an excursion with a view–the planning stages of surprises.

2ⁿᵈ

HAPPINESS IS . . . living out loud.

This doesn't necessarily mean going around shouting at everyone within earshot, per se. It simply means that my psyche should be gregarious, open and accepting...ready and willing to embrace the day/week/month/year with gusto. And right now, that's exactly what I'm trying to do.

3rd

HAPPINESS IS . . . starting the day on a positive note to lead me into a fruitful and affirming week.

4th

HAPPINESS IS . . . keeping my complaints to a minimum, putting my big girl panties on and just sucking it up.

MORE HAPPINESS IS . . . getting more satisfaction out of doing for others than you do waiting for others to do for you.

5th

HAPPINESS IS . . . a sense of belonging.

MORE HAPPINESS IS . . . realizing that I can't save the world, but taking care of myself and my contentment is totally within my grasp.

6th

HAPPINESS IS . . . waking up this morning and realizing that I'm pleased with the person I was yesterday, excited to make myself an even better person today and looking forward to the best person I can become tomorrow.

MORE HAPPINESS IS . . . finding pleasure in the simple things like watching chipmunks race about in the garden.

7th

HAPPINESS IS . . . defining my life by my actions and not being led by the exploits of others.

8th

HAPPINESS IS . . . my hubby.

> *On Monday, Oct. 3, I began suffering from a headache. By Thursday, that headache turned into a migraine. It's been an excruciating journey. Maarten has taken care of me today—to the point where he has essentially held me hostage in the house because he didn't want me to go outside and risk exacerbating the migraine. He coddled me, cuddled with me and brought me cups of hot tea and English muffins in bed. With his constant streams of "Baby can I get you this?" and "Baby can I get you that?" he personified the vow of 'in sickness and in health' in every way.*

9th

HAPPINESS IS . . . an appreciation for life's blessings, big and small, and giving thanks to the one who bestows them.

MORE HAPPINESS IS . . . being migraine-free.

10th

HAPPINESS IS . . . taking time out to not only smell the roses but to eat a few as well.

11th

HAPPINESS IS . . . moving on, putting a 'period' at the end of it and getting on with life.

> *This just seemed appropriate to me today. Many thanks to the cranky but loveable Judge Judith Sheindlin who always manages to dispense wise, sage advice in her own indelible way.*

> *Yesterday, I had a conversation with one of my sisters who inquired about my situation with the friend who mysteriously disappeared from my life back in August. I explained everything to her and told her that I just didn't have room in my heart—at least not yet—to reach out to accept her back as a friend after she painted me in such a horrible light and, essentially, abandoned me. She hurt me and that hurt can't be undone with a few words. There's no need to add drama and complication to my life. So for now, there will be one less friend in my life.*

> *Thanks, Judge Judy, for speaking your mind, telling it like it is and prompting me to put a period on that one.*

MORE HAPPINESS IS . . . less grumbling. Complaining is way overrated.

12th

HAPPINESS IS . . . constantly looking over my shoulder but only so I can see the good things I'm leaving behind–the same things that lead me to a better future.

13th

HAPPINESS IS . . . respecting your right to your opinions, views and beliefs (religious, political or otherwise, no matter how divergent from mine) and remaining free from mockery and disdain–and respectfully expecting the same from you.

MORE HAPPINESS IS . . . a state of being, of which I am the governor.

In my state, this state of happiness, I am the governor. I'm feeling slightly silly right now, but that's perfectly okay. As governor, I'm allowed.

14th

HAPPINESS IS . . . not saying "Oh I wish I could do the things that you do," to someone but, instead, doing it myself. The biggest thrill in life is living it!

While this isn't something that I just realized, it did dawn on me once again that I have no reason to envy what anyone else does or has in life. I live a very good life. I have a phenomenal husband who loves me very much, he makes it possible for me to have a lot in life–quite honestly, things that I wouldn't be able to have on my own–and together we are unstoppable. If I really want to travel, I can and do. If I want to buy a pair of boots or two (or three or four), I can and do.

But unlike some, I won't allow myself to give in to excesses. Yes, there are things that I wish I could do at times, but I can't. There are places where I yearn to travel, but sometimes the money's not right. But that doesn't mean I'm precluded from ever doing that. I can still do. And that knowledge is what keeps me from saying "I wish" and lets me know that, one day, "I will."

15th

HAPPINESS IS . . . growing, Growing, GROWN. One should never underestimate the awesomeness of a woman fully grown!

I am a woman, fully grown. I have been for quite some time now. This isn't a new revelation, but I just thought I'd remind a few folks who seem to think that I am a child to be trifled with. Now ya' know.

16th

HAPPINESS IS . . . looking up and giving praise to God, the one that made my life possible.

17th

HAPPINESS IS . . . channeling my inner Job for patience and my outer Don King for pure aesthetics as I continue to take these braids out of my hair (14 hours and counting...).

I started the long and tedious process of taking my braids out at one-thirty yesterday afternoon. Aside from a half hour break for dinner, I worked relentlessly until two o'clock in the wee hours of this morning. A mere six and a half hours later, I was up and at it again.

It's approximately ten-thirty in the morning as I write this. My fingers are cramping, I have a headache from all of the tugging on my head and I'm only a little over half way finished. But I will persevere. I have to. I have no choice. I need to finish what I've started.

Postscript: Finally, at eleven at night, my ordeal is over. All of the one hundred and one gazillion braids have been fastidiously yanked from my head one by one, the arduous task of combing the wild locks free of tangles is over and the comforting folds and familiar lumps of my mattress are calling my name. I'm coming bed...I'm coming.

18th

HAPPINESS IS . . . when desires become acquainted with goals, they marry and, together, give birth to a dream that is a reality.

19th

HAPPINESS IS . . . a yucky rainy day, chai tea, a comfy bed, my pooch and exercising my right to do absolutely nothing all day.

20th

HAPPINESS IS . . . getting ready 'cause while tomorrow isn't promised to me, I think I hear it calling my name.

21st

HAPPINESS IS . . . a very early start to the day and for good reason. Hello, my future. It's so nice to make your acquaintance.

22nd

HAPPINESS IS . . . great expectations…manifested.

23rd

HAPPINESS IS . . . basking in the afterglow of the fantastic Boney James concert last night at the Lyman Center.

24th

HAPPINESS IS . . . never ever losing sight of the value of memories of a departed loved one. Through it all I am still somehow able to smile through the tears.

25th

HAPPINESS IS . . . celebrating in the success of another on a major coup in her writing career and hoping, when the time comes, others will do the same for me when I hit my mark.

26th

HAPPINESS IS . . . believing in myself, even when no one else does.

27th

HAPPINESS IS . . . change.

Change is challenging, but change can be good.

28th

HAPPINESS IS . . . priceless snuggle time with the pooch on a cold autumn morning.

I woke up this morning to NBC Connecticut's headline lauding "Freak October Snow Eyes Connecticut" which led to an article screaming about a historic snow storm that could hit, possibly dumping a foot of snow in parts of the state.

Snow? Really? A foot? It's bad enough that at seven thirty-eight a.m. on October 28 it's only thirty-one degrees outside. Not only was I cold, but Kenji was so cold, he somehow managed to wiggle himself under the covers beside me. On top of the covers is fine, but under the covers? He shouldn't be under the covers. But he looked so precious laying there, his belly rising and falling ever so slightly as he snored lightly. I didn't have the heart to kick him out of the bed. So, instead, I snuggled with him.

29th

HAPPINESS IS . . . snow...not!

30th

HAPPINESS IS . . . being blessed.

As I awoke this morning through a cloud of red wine from the night before, I knew that life was good. I have to count my blessings. Not many people can live the kind of life that I do. I'm almost afraid to say this out loud or to even acknowledge it in words on a page for fear or being lambasted for actually enjoying the fruits of our labor. But my husband works hard to provide for both of us and, in my own way, I work hard as well. So why not enjoy ourselves?

I acknowledge the blessings. I don't count myself as lucky. I know where my blessings come from. I have a belief in God, the one and only Almighty, the ruler of my life. I may not acknowledge His presence in my life as often as I should, but I know and believe in His existence. And I know that, through His blessings, I exist. So to God be the glory. For my blessings in life. For my life. For my husband. And for being. That's a blessing all by itself.

31st

HAPPINESS IS . . . resisting the urge to slap myself silly because I'm just that happy with my life right now.

NOVEMBER

(With the trees almost stripped bare of their leaves, November straddles the line of Autumn and Winter, and was named the ninth month ["novem"] on the ancient Roman calendar)

1st

HAPPINESS IS . . . cherishing today and praying for tomorrow.

2nd

HAPPINESS IS . . . putting up or shutting up.

3ʳᵈ

HAPPINESS IS . . . difficult to achieve when turmoil and despair invade your life, but turning to God gives me much-needed solace.

I received terrible and disturbing news about a dear friend in Chicago yesterday. This feeling of helplessness is overwhelming because there is nothing that I can do to help the situation.

With each piece of information that is funneled down to me, the situation seems to grow more dire and bleaker. I can pray...but not much else. Sometimes prayer is all we have. But still, I've never felt so helpless.

4ᵗʰ

HAPPINESS IS . . . gettin' out of dodge for a brief respite.

I'll be flying the friendly skies today to meet up with Maarten in Dallas, TX. This will be my inaugural visit to the city and I'm looking forward to it. There's no trace of shame or trepidation as I freely admit that I plan to purposefully and systematically eat my way across the Dallas landscape.

5ᵗʰ

HAPPINESS IS . . . the art of adventure.

Today is the day for wandering around Texas. Where we'll end up is anybody's guess, but it feels great to just jump in the car and go.

6th

HAPPINESS IS . . . getting the inspiration to write...anywhere, anytime, anyplace.

The inspiration for a blog post cropped up as a result of a brief conversation at dinner last night. While the subject–referring to myself as a food writer as opposed to a food critic–was not a heated one, it started me thinking. Consequently, I felt compelled to set the record straight as to why I don't refer to myself as a food "critic" and why I'm perfectly happy being a food writer.

෯ ෯ ෯

"Me...a Restaurant Critic? Really? Pfftth"

Last night my husband and I had dinner with my friend Rosemary and her beau Scott at a tony restaurant in the Uptown section of Dallas. The food was delicious and the ambience was chic with a trendy vibe. An integral component of the dining experience was the service we received from our waiter, which was slightly above average. He went out of his way to engage us in conversation, spoke to us briefly about the evening's specials and even made drink suggestions when it seemed we were headed down the wrong path of imbibing.

These are my personal observations and interpretations of this restaurant. And this is what I do. I experience the entirety. What I don't do, however, is call myself a restaurant critic.

During dinner, Scott posed a question to me: "If you don't call yourself a restaurant critic, then what are you?"

After explaining to him exactly what I do, he followed up his question with what I found to be a very curious statement. "Then you need to define what it is you do...what you call yourself."

This was not something that I had to think long and hard about. I *know* what I do. I responded, "I'm a food writer."

Like most people, Scott believed a food critic and food writer to be wholly synonymous. I couldn't disagree more. In short, a critic scrutinizes and rates. As a food writer, I relate my overall dining experience sans ratings. My impressions, if you will.

A food or restaurant critic usually employs a rating system of some sort. One to four stars, smiley faces or, in the case of my early blog posts and then-reviews, one to five forks. I have since abandoned the practice of ratings for one primary and crucial reason: It's extremely subjective and not entirely reliable.

On a secondary note, restaurant ratings can have an adverse effect on not only an establishment's credibility but a proprietor's livelihood. All it takes is for a handful of people to see that Chez Blah-Blah restaurant has received one lousy star and word could spread like wildfire (because, as humans, we can be influenced by the silliest of things). Pretty soon, folks stop walking through the doors of Chez Blah-Blah, business falls off and, finally, they have to close their doors. Do I want that much responsibility? Hell no. I just want to write about food.

I write about my impressions and overall experience when dining out. Good or bad, it is what it is. I have *never* held myself out to be a food critic.

Do I make multiple visits to a restaurant before writing a review? Generally, no. As a freelance writer, I'm working from my own personal budget, not that of a major publication that reimburses me for every meal. Unfortunately, the luxury of spending money hand over fist at the same restaurant on two or three separate occasions before I say in print "I like this place" or, conversely "I don't like this place" isn't a necessity. Once again, I write based on my impressions of a restaurant at that present time–in the moment–and usually the need for multiple visits isn't necessary. This holds true particularly when, for one reason or another, the restaurant didn't offer an enjoyable experience. Honestly, why go back time and time again to someplace if I find a) the food distasteful; b) the staff rude; or c) the price point out of synch with the value of the experience? That would be akin to revisiting the same doctor who botched up your heart transplant surgery by removing your liver instead.

"Many food critics pursue professional experience in the world of food, attending culinary schools, working in restaurants, participating in farming, and so forth, so that they can learn about every aspect of the food industry. A good food critic is extremely knowledgeable about every aspect of food, from how certain foods are harvested to the history of various dishes. Food critics also have very well-developed palates, and they may

specialize in a particular area, such as traditional French cuisine, fusion cuisine, or so forth."

(Quoted from www.wisegeek.com article, 'What Is a Food Critic?')

As a humble food writer, I have not amassed this type of experience. And this is not a putdown of myself. I love me and just won't stand for such nonsense. So what qualifies me to write about food, you ask? Simply put, I love food. I love everything about it:

- the enticing aromas that tickle my nostrils;
- the aesthetic beauty that has me eating with my eyes long before a morsel reaches my mouth;
- the enthralling flavors that play on my taste buds;
- the many and varied textures the be felt with the hands and mouth; and
- the medley of sounds that food can make, from the sizzling of fajita meat on a hot skillet to the crackly crunch of the well-seasoned skin of a duck breast.

I adore it all.

It is for all these reasons and more that I choose to write about food. So call me what you will: food writer, culinary writer, food impressionist. But please don't call me a critic because that's not who I am. I'm proud to call myself a food writer. Maybe one day I'll rise to the ranks of food critic. But until that time, I'll continue to assault the world with my humble impressions of restaurants hither and yon. After all, it's not such a bad gig. The only major downfall is my ever-expanding waistline.

7th

HAPPINESS IS . . . going out on a limb and taking chances.

8th

HAPPINESS IS . . . homeward-bound.

It's been real, Dallas, but now it's time for me to board a plane for home. I must admit I enjoy everything about traveling: exploring someplace new, the adventure, seeing old friends and making new ones, the fabulous and sometimes not so fabulous cuisine. However, no matter where I go or for how long, I always miss my pooch! Mommy's coming home Kenji!

9th

HAPPINESS IS . . . Johannesburg, moving forward.

10th

HAPPINESS IS . . . dealing with disappointment gracefully.

This is much easier said than done, but I do try.

11th

HAPPINESS IS . . . family - the unexpected gifts in your life.

It's only for a short while, but I'm grateful for my sister Wanda's visit to Stamford. For so many years, when I lived in Atlanta, I tried to get my family to visit me. In twenty years, I could count on one hand the number of times that any one family member boarded a plan in Maryland and made the six hundred mile trek to the South to see me.

After a while, I simply gave up. My resolve was spent. There would be no more cajoling, no more whining, no more pouting. I would suffer in silence, never again letting on how I really felt about my family's lack of presence in my life. Of course, I saw them all the time, but it was because I took the initiative to hop on a plane to visit them.

Now that my husband and I live much closer to my family, my assumption was that I would see them more often. However, aside from the entire contingent driving here for my husband's surprise birthday party and the one time when my dad, one of my sisters and her boyfriend came to take care of me during my breast cancer scare, my assumption was correct. However, once again it was because I was the one loading up the car and driving the two hundred plus miles to see them.

That all changed yesterday when Wanda arrived. She came to see me for no particular reason other than she just wanted to spend time with me.

That makes me happy and bears repeating. It makes me happy.

12th

HAPPINESS IS . . . when good times and great people collide.

13th

HAPPINESS IS . . . spending the day in NYC with my sister.

And what a great day it was. We saw the play "The Mountaintop" starring Samuel L. Jackson and Angela Bassett, shopped at the Bryant Park Holiday Shops, marveled at the sometimes tawdry sometimes brash but always fascinating lights of Times Square and dined at Pershing Square Café. By the end of the day, our tired and worn bodies knew we had experienced something wonderful and special that can only be shared by sisters.

14th

HAPPINESS IS . . . squeezing the most out of the time we have, sharing a laugh with those close to your heart and short goodbyes.

Wanda left today to go back home to Maryland. Even the dog was saddened by her departure. He sulked around the house for hours after she left. Yeah, I know the feeling, Kenji.

15th

HAPPINESS IS . . . trusting that your accomplishments can be amazing if you believe in yourself.

16th

HAPPINESS IS . . . waiting patiently to reenact the infamous scene from "A Few Good Men" in court. I am so ready for my close-up Mr. DeMille.

Jury duty.

Do I have a screw loose or what? I was actually looking forward to jury duty, even though I loathed the fact that I had to set my alarm for seven o'clock in the morning to make it to the courthouse by eight-thirty. I don't do mornings. But the anticipation was killing me. And it all turned out to be for naught because the anticlimactic pinnacle of the morning was enough to deflate my self-imposed high.

As part of the potential jury pool, we watched a brief video on the voir dire process and my hopes soared. After the video, nine individuals were called to the front of the room. I was among that small group and as I walked towards the podium, I beamed. I was going to be among the first to begin the process.

"Okay, you can go," the stern looking diminutive woman said flatly.

"Go where? To another room?" I asked dumbfounded.

"No, you can leave. Go home."

I was stunned. It wasn't even nine-thirty and I was being kicked out of the courthouse without so much as an invasive line of questioning by a crabby judge or an overzealous attorney.

Well just damn. Maybe I wanted jury duty too bad. That's just wrong on so many levels.

17th

HAPPINESS IS . . . finishing all of my Christmas shopping one week before Thanksgiving! Woooo Hooooo!!! Merry Christmas!

MORE HAPPINESS IS . . . the power of "I am."

I walked into the living room, where I had left the television set blaring so the dog would have something to look at while I worked in the office, and Dr. Phil had just sat down with Joel Olsteen for a chat.

Joel started off by asserting that there is so much power in simply saying "I am" – "I am attractive," "I am successful," or whatever it is that affirms our station in life. It is akin to the power of prayer. That was a very powerful and profound statement in the mere space of two words.

Simply wonderful and wonderfully simple.

I am. Are you?

18th

HAPPINESS IS . . . believing enough in myself so that I can step my big foot forward and make the statement "Here I am, world! Accept me as I am and as I evolve; take it or leave it."

I'm feeling very 'me' today. And more power to me. None of this moping around feeling sorry for myself about…whatever. It's a gorgeous day outside and God has seen fit to awaken me to all that it has to offer. Who am I to turn my back on that?

MORE HAPPINESS IS . . . keeping a smile plastered on my face even while I have one good nerve left allocated for the day and someone is seriously plucking it.

19th

HAPPINESS IS . . . homecomings.

20th

HAPPINESS IS . . . having and maintaining a positive outlook (I'm positive I'm going to overeat on Thanksgiving).

21st

HAPPINESS IS . . . sharing.

MORE HAPPINESS IS . . . the good old days and the friends that remind you of them.

> Today, my friend Nina took me on a short jaunt down memory lane. A simple thought struck her as so comical that she called to tell me of her recollection. Together, we laughed as we reminisced about the icy incident that occurred many years before at the Addison Road subway station parking lot. While it has absolutely no meaning to anyone else, for us it was simply hilarious. Thank you, Nina, for keeping the good old days alive and kicking.

22nd

HAPPINESS IS . . . having a long drawn out conversation with myself, with the requisite back-and-forth pros and cons, before at long last coming to this realization: I'm not going to respond to you, oh negative energy vampire, because it's not worth the aggravation. Part of growing is learning to move past the negative.

23rd

HAPPINESS IS . . . the nuts and bolts, ins and outs, highs and lows of preparing for Thanksgiving dinner with the family—all of which will undoubtedly lead to more than one tryptophan comatose episode and sweet potato pie overload.

MORE HAPPINESS IS . . . remembering my Mom on this day of her birth.

24th

HAPPINESS IS . . . a wonderful day filled with family, good food, giving thanks and a prayer for lost loved ones.

Isn't that what Thanksgiving is all about?

25th

HAPPINESS IS . . . life's unexpected blessings.

26th

HAPPINESS IS . . . working in the kitchen nonstop for three and a half hours with my sister as we prepare a big brunch for the entire family. Lots of work but it brings many rewards.

27th

HAPPINESS IS . . . four hours door-to-door from daddy's house to our house; a new record!

28th

HAPPINESS IS . . . laughing so hard with total strangers this morning that I actually snorted and didn't care.

29th

HAPPINESS IS . . . radical thoughts to keep life exciting!

30th

HAPPINESS IS . . . honing my craft.

Today is dedicated to doing research on the various alternative publishing models. While I would love to have my books published in the traditional manner, there's no time like the present to give thought to other avenues that will allow for getting my work out there.

DECEMBER

(Cold winds blow, winter descends across the land, the season of Advent begins, and The Yule Log program graces our TV screens on Christmas morning along with classic holiday music. December, the holy month, marks the birth month of Jesus)

1st

HAPPINESS IS . . . doing in life what I believe I was destined to do.

I am doing my calling. At least that's what I truly believe in my heart.

I believe it was God's will for me to write. He gave me this gift. I don't make any claims to be the best that there is at this wonderful craft of writing, but it is what it is. And it's the one thing that's for me and me alone that makes me feel special.

It rises far above the level of just finding something at which to be good. For each and every one of us, I believe there are things in life that we are chosen and called upon to do. It's those things that are our natural fit; our gift. This belongs to me.

How wasteful it would be of me not to nurture such a glorious gift.

MORE HAPPINESS IS . . . done.

It's three minutes past eleven in the evening and I've just completed proofing my book, "From City to Safari: One Woman's Exploration of Johannesburg, South Africa." It was a long, arduous process, but I'm excited about this turning point in my life. It means I've moved from "I want to" to "I did."

2nd

HAPPINESS IS . . . that comfortable place somewhere between "I'm feeling good" and "I'm deliriously ecstatic" where I try to reside every day.

3rd

HAPPINESS IS . . . reflecting on those who are no longer friends in life and realizing that my life is probably richer, fuller and simply better without them.

4th

HAPPINESS IS . . . embracing emotional growth and discovering that the woman I am today is only half the person I plan to be tomorrow.

5th

HAPPINESS IS . . . jumping over the hurdles placed in your path to fulfill your dreams.

MORE HAPPINESS IS . . . agreeing with anyone who believes I CAN'T do something. To me, it means I "Can *Achieve Numerous Things*"! You *CANT* too!

6th

HAPPINESS IS . . . shaking off the bad and donning the lovely.

7th

HAPPINESS IS . . . learning and living a life lesson: setbacks aren't show stoppers; they're merely speed bumps that slow you down and help you focus.

Someone has let me down. While trying to achieve a dream, it has been deferred slightly because of disappointment. I try not to become hardened when such things occur.

I suppose I should adopt the view that the only person I can and should truly depend on in life is myself, but I know that, for me, those would be empty words. Such a hard-line stance is difficult for me to adopt because it goes against my intrinsic need to believe in the good in everyone. Well, nearly everyone.

So I must adjust. Adjust to the malfeasance of others. Modify my thinking so as not to allow the letdown be the end-all. Did I bounce back from today's descent? I've moved on to Plan B. Hopefully, success will prevail. Only time will tell.

8th

HAPPINESS IS . . . calming myself and self-correcting in the face of uncertainty.

Yesterday, I was upset because I felt let down by a friend. Today, I had to question not only my motives for being troubled but also my response to the lack of communication on her part. The fact of the matter is I didn't respond–I reacted, which is rarely a good thing. Reaction breeds assumptions which can often be false, and I don't want to be guilty of falling into that trap.

The reality of what is transpiring could be far different than anything my mind may be conjuring up at this time. Putting aside my feelings, there are a myriad of possibilities that need to be considered: perhaps something has happened to my friend. Maybe she is in some sort of trouble or dealing with strife in her life that far surpasses my needs which, in the grand scheme of things, are trivial.

Yes, I have self-corrected. I was being selfish. The entire story is unknown to me at this time. To be unresponsive to my numerous inquiries...this is unlike my friend. I cannot take it for granted that she would purposely choose to ignore me without a good reason. So I wait. Instead of fabricating motives, reasons or excuses, my patience will prevail. Sooner or later, the answers will come. At that time, I'll know how to appropriately respond. She is, after all, my friend. Despite this bump in the road, that hasn't changed.

MORE HAPPINESS IS . . . done; no seriously, I mean it's really done this time and about a week away from the big reveal.

Tonight my latest book, "From City to Safari: One Woman's Exploration of Johannesburg, South Africa" was finalized and published. I'm waiting for it to appear on Amazon and then I can tell the world. This. Is. Heaven.

9th

HAPPINESS IS . . . making a tall refreshing glass of lemonade from all of these lemons that life has been giving me lately.

As I sat in the terminal awaiting my Delta flight to Atlanta which would eventually lead me to Greensboro, NC, I couldn't help but reflect on the obstacles that have cropped up in my path. Had I been a quitter, I would have allowed myself to be beat down by those temporary setbacks. But oh contraire...I am no quitter.

Defeat is not easily had in my world and I am not one to accept it quietly and meekly; I face it head on–kicking, screaming and, at times, biting. So when I am, in fact, conquered, know that it was a hard fought battle that I engaged in and giving in easily was not an option. And in defeat, there's always the promise of victory the next time around.

10th

HAPPINESS IS . . . the pride and emotion of witnessing my nephew graduate from college. Congratulations Earlie Clark IV, the world's newest engineer, on this momentous occasion!

Today, my twenty-three year old nephew graduated from North Carolina A&T in Greensboro, NC with a Bachelors of Science in Mechanical Engineering. Talk about beaming with pride!

11th

HAPPINESS IS . . . leaving the irritating chronic complaining to the irritating chronic complainers.

12th

HAPPINESS IS . . . rolling right along.

13th

HAPPINESS IS . . . keeping the momentum going.

14th

HAPPINESS IS . . . crack o' dawn writing.

It's six in the morning. I've been awake since four and I've been downstairs in the office writing since five. No time like the present to write. And so I write. "Peace Be With Us" is on my mind and on my computer screen. The act of recapturing what was once lost is a tiresome one. I'm on page thirty-one of two hundred and fifty, however, I won't look at it as having a long way to go but rather as having gotten a bit under my belt. Onward and upward.

MORE HAPPINESS IS . . . donning my culinary mad scientist robe and creating in the kitchen.

EVEN MORE HAPPINESS IS . . . after so many years, beginning to recapture the greatness that was once lost but never forgotten.

Yesterday was a new beginning. A manuscript that fell prey to the perils of a computer crash is being reborn.

Yesterday, I began working once again on "Peace Be With Us," to regain what was lost. I feel a great sense of accomplishment at this very moment. Although it was a dream deferred, I didn't allow my dream to totally falter. Now, as I continue with the process of restoring the story that was once lost, I have a sense of renewal. I can do this. I can do this.

15th

HAPPINESS IS . . . shaking off the bad to make more room for the good.

My mind wanders. Of course, sometimes I don't want it to go on the journey that it seems destined to take. It's at times like these that being—and staying—positive is a true asset. I can't pay myself lip service. I need to be about what I speak about. So when that hoped-for show of support for the milestones that I accomplish doesn't materialize, the answer is not to wallow in my own misery. Instead, I have to allow optimistic thoughts to be my guide.

We all want to be encouraged in life; it allows us to feel more motivated, more compelled to move forward, more driven. Yet there are those who feel that perhaps this is not needed—this affirmation of a job well done. Some find it difficult to give praise. I believe I am the exact opposite. If I extend my hand to someone, tomorrow someone else may extend their hand to me. It's this chain of facilitation that bears witness to a spirit of comfort that lets us, as humans, know that we are not totally alone in what we do.

Whether or not I have a cheering section is secondary. Do I want one? Of course. And ultimately, from those in my life who truly matter, I can say that I do have a small but powerful rallying force behind me. So today, I vow to shake off these melancholy feelings in lieu of the good things that are bound to come my way. In the end, by the grace of God, I rise and fall on my own merits.

MORE HAPPINESS IS . . . change is afoot.

I'm finally ready to redo my professional website. We'll see what transpires over the course of the next few weeks. This could be a disaster in the making...

16th

HAPPINESS IS . . . change, once again.

Today I begin the process of change...of my website, that is. Before long, GoDaddy will be a thing of the past. Hello "Sky" WordPress theme! Once again, it's the little things that make me happy.

17th

HAPPINESS IS . . . trying desperately to find one shred of a happy thought at this precise moment of extreme frustration—but still I smile through the "grrrrrr".

This whole DIY website s**t is not working very well for me. I can't believe I'm on the verge of tears, but I am. The level of aggravation is such that I want to pick up my computer, snap it in half with my bare hands and eat it. There has got to be a better way.

18th

HAPPINESS IS . . . a week before Santa's official visit and I'm so excited.

For the first time ever, since meeting my then-future-husband in 2007, we're finally spending Christmas together. Life, family obligations and plain old stuff just got in the way. Now, after being apart in body but together in spirit four years in a row, this is the year that, instead of me being in Maryland with my family and he with his family all the way in Voorhout, I'll be able to come downstairs...in my home...on Christmas morning...and spend it with Maarten.

19th

HAPPINESS IS . . . bringing it down a notch, tackling the hiccups in the road and vowing to be the strength to a friend in need.

How easy it would be for me to feel sorry for myself, even though whatever it is that I perceive as ailing me is rather tiny. But I need to be there for others. For someone in particular. She needs my strength.

20th

HAPPINESS IS . . . knowing that the right words at the right time by the right person make all the difference.

I had a chat with a friend today. Without realizing it when the chat began, it was just what I needed to give me a much needed boost. She helped me to put certain events that are taking place in my life right now in clear perspective, to find and hold onto the strength that I need to be the pillar for someone else and to remain strong even when I think I'm not doing enough.

And now I'm calling you out: Thank you, Shimah.

21st

HAPPINESS IS . . . searching for and finding it every day.

22nd

HAPPINESS IS . . . after a few days of being out of sorts, out of energy and out of steam, finally finding my way back to the land of the living.

23rd

HAPPINESS IS . . . knowing that it isn't about me all the time and being gracious enough to accept that.

I received a heartbreaking telephone call last night. And while I did manage to sleep for six undisturbed hours–and feeling pangs of guilt for having done so–I did cry myself to sleep. The mother of a very close friend has passed away. It's not simply dealing with the loss of her that is causing grief, but the circumstances that led up to her passing. Whether it is an untimely demise or not is yet to be seen. And therein is the crux of this distressing problem.

I prayed before I climbed into bed last night. I prayed for my friend who is, at this moment, separated from her loved ones. Lonely and alone, I feel helpless in helping her. But I'm a firm believer in the power of prayer.

Keep her safe, Lord.

24th

HAPPINESS IS . . . early to bed, early to rise, makes a woman...oh, I'll cut the crap! It's just great to be alive!

25th

HAPPINESS IS . . . the reason for the season. Merry Christmas.

26th

HAPPINESS IS . . . over the river and through the woods...and zipping across the friendly skies across the pond...to the in-laws house we go!

27th

HAPPINESS IS . . . planes, trains and automobiles.

From start to finish, our trip involved Stamford, New York, London, Dusseldorf and Voorhout, and included two planes, five trains and four automobiles. But we did it....we made it to Holland safe and sound. Phew! Where to next?

28th

HAPPINESS IS . . . winding down one year and gearing up for the new year approaching.

29th

HAPPINESS IS . . . being grateful that mine is not a temperament of perpetual negativity and not being conditioned to a state of misery.

30th

HAPPINESS IS . . . preparing to say goodbye to the last of the three hundred sixty-five...

December 31st

HAPPINESS IS . . . a stroll through the village.

In The Netherlands, they take the celebration of the New Year to a-whole-nother level. Fireworks are BIG over here. They've been shooting them off for a couple of days now...but today folks have lost their freakin' minds! Sounds like warfare out there now but tonight will be like Afghanistan.

What a wonderful way to prepare to bring in 2012. As I get ready for the auspicious occasion this evening, when my Dutch family will gather around the dining table and enjoy a fabulous spread, there are thoughts of my family back home in Maryland. Although far away at the moment, they're dear to my heart now, as always.

What a year. There have been many ups and downs—some pivotal which marked a turning point in my life, while others were mere blips on the radar that are long since forgotten. But through it all, I've tried to maintain a sense of stability in my life, that fine line called balance that sees us teetering on one side or the other of good or not so good.

It seems fitting to end the year engaging in the things that bring so much joy to my life: traveling, eating and writing. On this last day of

2011, my final words that propel me forward to another year are those that rejoice in the beauty of family.

"Out With The Old (Food) And In With The New" was my final blog post of the year and it celebrated the here and now. There will be many more here and now moments to come, but for now, I revel in what is current. And I feel blessed that I have been able to recapture the very essence of happiness throughout this past year. Life isn't perfect, but it is my life. And for what it's worth, I'm happy.

ल ल ल

"Out With The Old (Food) And in With The New"

This past year has been one of a varied, if not a tremendous, culinary voyage for me. I've experienced delicious fare at pubs and restaurants throughout England, and, most notably, at the home of my friend Karen in Rawdon where sweet and savory baked chicken was on the menu. My dining proclivities led me to Dallas where, despite the sumptuous and pricey meal at a tony restaurant, the evening was not without interlopers which crawled about in the form of ants parading across our crisp white linen tablecloth. I have even had the occasion to pamper myself with delicate handmade crab and shrimp ravioli adorned with flying fish roe alongside a generously sized rock lobster tail–not once but twice–on the lovely island of Barbados.

So it would seem fitting that, instead of ending the year on a culinary note that my palate is duly accustomed to–dare I say the same old same old–I close out 2011 and ring in 2012 with a tradition that, while not culturally inherent to me, is such for those who are near and dear to me.

Just minutes before midnight, on December 31, 2011, as I sit at the carefully adorned table of my in-laws home in the tiny village of Voorhout in the South Holland province of The Netherlands, my eyes sweep over the evening's modest feast that, to most Americans, would be an appetizer to an otherwise more expansive spread. The food that makes up the snackfest are mostly what is desired at the time. For us, my Dutch family, there is no real rhyme or reason to the varied dishes spread around the table.

From crab claw fingers marinated in olive oil and garlic to smoked salmon to delicious cheeses straight from the kaasboer (cheese farmer) one village over, and even spinach and salmon filled pastries alongside stuffed tomatoes that sit across the table from tiny cubes of curry chicken, the occasion is not so much about the pickings themselves but the ones with whom you share the pickings. That is, however, with the exception of a true Dutch New Year's favorite.

Two traditional pastries favored by the Dutch for their annual New Year's celebration are once again on hand for our consumption. Oliebollen, deep fried balls of dough, are essentially the cousin to donuts, and Appelflappen, battered and deep fried apple treats, are both deliciously difficult to resist. I'm almost certain that at this very minute, hundreds upon thousands of Dutch men, women and children are indulging in one or the other—or both—of these time-honored goodies and lovin' every bite.

Make no mistake about it: oliebollen is a greasy concoction that, if eaten in heavy doses, could coat your stomach worse than gobbling down a bucket of The Colonel's own fried chicken. But who gives a damn about decorum when you have something that is so decadent? True oliebollen comes in two varieties: plain or with raisins. While you may fare a bit better in the grease department by choosing a golden brown appelflappen fritter over oliebollen, what you save in oil you'll surely make up for in calories because, just like Lay's potato chips, you can't eat just one. And to make oliebollen and appelflappen even more tempting, shake a generous amount of powdered sugar over the top and you're living in style just like a true Dutch person.

New Year's Eve is a festive occasion for the people of The Netherlands. The celebratory nature of the holiday brings about the boom of fireworks long before the clock strikes midnight. But once that magical hour hits, you'll want to step outside to gaze up at the night sky which is filled with colorful light shows that rival Independence Day celebrations in the United States.

The Dutch New Year's Eve meal is a simple one. But for the people of The Netherlands, it is shared with family and friends—those we hold dear to our hearts.

As people the world over say goodbye to the old year and welcome the new one with open arms, in Holland too we share in this passage of time as we toast with a bottle of champagne, watch the magnificent and colorful fireworks displays and say Gelukkig Nieuw Jaar.

And from me to you, whatever the year 2011 held for you–whether filled with joy, pain, trials and tribulations, success, surprises, disappointment, dreams fulfilled and more–may 2012 be far greater than you could ever imagine. Think big...dream big...live big...and eat well.

Happy New Year!

ABOUT THE AUTHOR

VALERIE ALBARDA is an author and freelance writer whose books include *From City to Safari: One Woman's Exploration of Johannesburg, South Africa* and *An Affair to Remember: Bellissimo Italia*

Valerie has an almost insatiable love of traveling and cuisine. Her articles have appeared on such sites as *WomanAroundTown.com*, an online woman's lifestyle magazine and *Stamford.Patch.com*, an online community news source, as well as on her own blog, *Bon Vivant*. She also pens two food-centric columns for a local news website. Her itinerant nature has led her on journeys to various countries on at least three continents...so far.

Gettin' Back to Happy is inspired by her desire to restore a sense of happiness to her life through the simple act of evoking at least one positive thought a day.

Valerie calls Stamford, CT home along with her globetrotting Dutch husband and blonde lab-mix dog.
For more information on Valerie, visit her website at
www.ValerieAlbarda.com.

www.ingramcontent.com/pod-product-compliance
Lightning Source LLC
Chambersburg PA
CBHW060255050426
42448CB00009B/1647